A. BELIEVER

JORDAN B. PETERSON'S CHRIST REVEALED

BEYOND BEYOND ORDER OR MAPS OF MEANING BY IMMERSION

Jordan B. Peterson's Christ Revealed

Beyond Beyond Order or Maps of Meaning by Immersion

©2022 Anonymous Believer

print ISBN: 978-1-66787-823-2

ebook ISBN: 978-1-66787-824-9

CONTENTS

INTRODUCTION

What's he pointing at?

Imagine you're dreaming and in your dream you see Jordan Peterson standing in a field on a moonless summer evening. You watch as he points to three particular stars and then uses his finger to trace the outline of a triangle whose vertices are defined by those three stars. After he has traced this outline a few times, he turns to you and says, "There, somewhere in that triangle. That's where you'll find it. It has to be there but I can't see it." Then, his eyes lock tightly on yours and he asks, "Can you see it?"

Instinctively, you look up and bring your gaze to the area defined by those three stars. At first, you see nothing either. You continue to stare into that space wondering what exactly Jordan Peterson expects to find there.

Get your story straight

Jordan Peterson (JP) first appeared on my radar at Thanksgiving[1] in 2018. I was almost immediately captivated by what I perceived to be the strength of his character and the soundness of his thinking, especially his ideas relating to the Bible. His lectures on the Bible left me wondering how someone could possibly approach Scripture from the scientific perspective and get so close to what Christians call sound doctrine. But to understand my fascination with JP's thinking you need to know a bit about my story.

Aim at something. Pick the best target you can currently concep-tualize. Stumble toward it. Notice your errors and misconceptions

---

1   That's the Canadian Thanksgiving, which is held on the second Monday in October.

along the way, face them, and correct them. **Get your story straight.** *Past, present, future—they all matter... For better or worse, you are on a journey. You are having an adventure—and your map better be accurate.*

– Beyond Order

I'm a bit less than two years younger than Jordan Peterson, which is to say I'm quickly approaching 60 and so my story had pretty much been played out already when I first encountered JP, four years ago. Despite my story having been mostly played out, and as strange as this might sound, JP's ideas would completely alter my understanding of my story. In fact, before JP, I was convinced that my story simply could not be set straight.

I'd given up on making sense of the journey that I had already travelled. My story, prior to encountering JP's ideas, consisted of three completely disjointed and, as far as I was concerned, unrelated pieces. The problem was that I'd started my story over from scratch, not once but twice, and that left my life split into three pieces that were, from my perspective, separate, stand-alone pieces, and most importantly, irreconcilable. These pieces bore more resemblance to a collection of slightly related short stories than anything even remotely resembling a single, cohesive, and coherent narrative. Attempting to make sense of the whole seemed impossible. Even now, in the light of hindsight, I can see that it actually would have been impossible to make sense of my story without Jordan Peterson's ideas. Allow me to give you an idea of why this was the case and to introduce you to the ideas that allowed me to finally get my story straight, the ideas that this book will center around.

Three distinct chapters

My life can be broken down into three distinct epochs or chapters, with each chapter covering a period of roughly twenty years. The first chapter is all about what Peterson calls "enculturation" or "adoption of a shared map." In my case, the culture in question was Catholic, Roman Catholic to be precise. As a result, the first chapter in my story was all about ritual, ceremony, customs, and traditions. That is, this chapter was about embodying my culture, absorbing its implicit beliefs through its various "symbols" and by acting out its particular rituals. I was entirely steeped in this culture. For example, not just one but both my parents attended mass religiously. What's more, my education was also Catholic. I attended Catholic schools, including an all-boy, strictly academic high school, where many of the teachers were priests and mass was observed during such times as lent. I went along with all of this until I left home, at nineteen.

The first chapter in my life, then, comes to an end when I stepped out into the world on my own. The line that separates the first and second chapters isn't crisp and clean. Instead, this line consists of a transition period that lasted somewhere between two and three years. During this period, I not only left home but got married, had a son, and witnessed my mother lose her battle to cancer (before my son's first birthday.) I was completely and utterly overwhelmed by life during this transition period.

It didn't take me long to realize that I had shipwrecked my life right from the very start. I had been poorly prepared for the reality that awaited me as I stepped out on my own and foolish enough to dive in head first. As a result, I found myself drowning, going under for the third time as it were. It was then that I "turned to Christ" for help. I abandoned my Catholic belief system to become a "Bible-believing" Christian. That is, I converted from Catholicism to the Protestant faith. I didn't do this by half-measures either. I went all-in, as they say.

> *The core idea is this: subjugate yourself voluntarily to a set of socially determined rules—those with some tradition in their formulation—and a unity that transcends the rules will emerge. That unity constitutes what you could be, if you concentrate on a particular goal and see it through.*
>
> – Beyond Order

I had no real idea of what I was doing but, in JP's terms what I did during the second chapter of my life corresponds to this idea of subjugating myself *voluntarily to a set of socially determined rules*. In my case, the *rules* consisted of the Bible itself. During this time, as a fundamentalist evangelical Christian, I read the Bible daily. What's more I spent a lot of time also studying the Bible and meditating on it. In fact, I became so familiar with the Bible that, on hearing a Biblical reference, I could bring to mind what book of the Bible it was from as well as summarize the context from which the quote was taken. And while I subjugated myself voluntarily to the teachings of the Bible, I would never have used the word "subjugation" to describe what I was doing, because this subjugation was done out of a heart of gratitude and not servitude. Regardless, I remained in this state of *voluntary subjugation* to the *set of rules* expressed in Scripture for nearly twenty years.

That leads us to the third chapter of my story. This is where the story goes off the rails. You see, at the age of forty, after having essentially lived my entire life from the religious perspective, I abruptly closed my Bible and walked away from God. As I'd done at the end of the first chapter of my life, I once again jettisoned my entire belief system. From this point on, the story—my story—stopped making sense. And it wouldn't make sense again until JP appeared on my radar fourteen years later and I'd become familiar enough with ideas to begin to see how the pieces fit together.

You can imagine my curiosity then, when I came across JP. The first thing that struck me was just how closely his ideas about the Bible mirrored my understanding of Scripture. The fact that here was a scientist who could expound on the Bible in such a way that it reminded me of some of the great preachers of my past was something incredibly strange for me. Here was an anomaly that didn't make sense to me, and it's precisely this that drew me to explore JP's ideas, especially his most fundamental ideas, the ones he cared enough about to put down in writing.

It's been four years since I first encountered JP's ideas. In that time, I've become very familiar with his thinking, which has in turn enabled me to get my story straight. It's been a slow and arduous process, however, because the more I became familiar with JP's ideas, the more I could see just how strange they were. At first, I made the mistake of thinking that I understood what he meant because he used a vocabulary that I was extremely familiar with. The more I paid attention to the details, however, the more I realized that while he was using familiar words, the meaning behind the words was very different—so different, in fact, that it required prolonged repeated exposure before I could stop seeing my ideas in his words so that I could start to see what he really meant by those words. This process culminated in a clear understanding of JP's conception of Christ which, as it turned out, was far stranger than I'd ever imagined when I first encountered his ideas.

And so, the primary objective of this book is to make what I've discovered visible to you. That is, the purpose of this book is to *reveal* what JP means by Christ and to do so in such a way that you can "see" it for yourself. I'm sure you'll be as surprised by what you see as I was.

Christ: The strange idea

JP's thinking is extremely complex and very abstract. As a result, I suspect that most people who listen to him have only a vague understanding of what he is saying. This is especially true when it comes to JP's conception of Christ. When JP uses the word "Christ," he means something very specific, something very precise, but the abstract nature of what he means by Christ makes getting a clear picture of what he's talking about nearly impossible. This is especially true if "Jesus" is standing in the way. What I mean by that is that it is especially difficult to see JP's conception of Christ if you have your own conception of Christ, because your conception of Christ is bound to prevent you from seeing his. This is especially true if you're a Christian. If, like most Westerners, you already have an idea of what Christ represents, you're likely to assume that there is significant overlap between your conception of Christ and JP's conception of Christ. If that's you, and you think JP's conception of Christ resembles yours, then you're in for quite a surprise. What I mean by that should become abundantly clear in Chapter 1.

Whether Christian or not, whatever you imagine that JP means by Christ, I can pretty well guarantee that it bears little resemblance to JP's actual conception of Christ. That is, JP's conception of Christ is truly "anomalous." What I mean by that is that JP's conception of Christ constitutes what JP calls a "Strange Idea" in *Maps of Meaning* (MoM) and, as such, it serves as the perfect springboard into a deeper exploration of JP's most fundamental ideas, those expressed in MoM, starting with what he means by anomaly. There are *four particular forms of anomaly* delineated in MoM. They are: *The Strange, the Stranger, the Strange Idea, and the Revolutionary Hero.* What's more, JP tells us that *anomalies manifest themselves on the border between chaos and order, so to speak, and have a threatening and promising aspect. He continues:*

> *The promising aspect dominates, when the contact is voluntary, when the exploring agent is up-to-date—when the individual has explored all previous anomalies, released the "information" they contained, and built a strong personality and steady "world" from that information. The threatening aspect dominates, when the contact is involuntary, when the exploring agent is not up-to-date—when the individual has run away from evidence of his previous errors, failed to extract the information "lurking behind" his mistakes, weakened his personality, and destabilized his "world." The phenomenon of interest—that precursor to exploratory behavior—signals the presence of a potentially "beneficial" anomaly.* **Interest manifests itself where an assimilable but novel phenomenon exists: where something new "hides," in a partially comprehensible form.** *Devout adherence to the dictates of interest—assuming a suitably disciplined character—therefore insures stabilization and renewal of personality and world.*
>
> – Maps of Meaning

This book treats JP's conception of Christ as a truly strange idea, in the MoM sense. There's *something new hiding* in JP's conception of Christ but it is currently expressed only in a *partially comprehensible form.* What we want to do is fully understand JP's conception of Christ and thereby *assimilate* the idea. In fact, this idea of assimilating JP's conception of Christ may be the closest thing to a concise summary of what this book is really about. Of course, before we can assimilate JP's conception of Christ, we first need to take what is currently expressed in a *partially comprehensible form* and render it *visible* or *fully comprehensible,* and that's no small feat.

Considering just how complex and abstract JP's thinking is in general, it should come as no surprise that it will take us two chapters to fully *reveal* what JP means by Christ. Once we're done, however, we will have a very clear picture of his conception of Christ. And armed with this *fully comprehensible form* of his conception of Christ, we'll be able to see just how strange an idea it truly is. At that point, we'll switch gears, as it were, in order to *assimilate* this strange idea. To achieve that we're going to weave in elements from my life's story as well as bring another of JP's four forms of anomaly into the spotlight: the Revolutionary Hero.

Anyone familiar with JP's books will be familiar with the story of Osiris, Seth, and Horus. He uses this story to illustrate the fundamental pattern that any individual or society experiences as a consequence of any *process of profound change.* The pattern itself is simple, "stable state, descent into chaos, reestablishment of stability."[2] There are, however, a few important elements to this pattern that the Egyptian myth reveals. In its mythological form, the descent into chaos, for instance consists of diving into the void or the abyss, sinking to the bottom and getting swallowed by a beast that lurks at the bottom of that abyss. The myth also informs us that if *the descent into chaos* is successful it will culminate in finding *"your dead father"* within the belly of that beast. The reestablishment of stability is represented mythological by the idea of revivifying this *dead father,* revivifying him and bringing

---

2   The fact of that depth means that such accounts can be used diversely as a meaningful frame for any process of profound change experienced by any individual or society (stable state, descent into chaos, reestablishment of stability), and can lend that process multidimensional reality, context, powerful meaning, and motivation. (*Beyond Order.*)

him back to the surface. These elements are all part of the general pattern of the hero's quest and the revolutionary hero is a particular incarnation of this pattern. We are, of course, merely introducing these ideas here.

Don't worry if you're currently unfamiliar with JP's most fundamental ideas. We'll be taking a close look at those ideas that most closely relate to his conception of Christ so that, when we're done, you'll not only have a clear picture of what JP means by Christ but you'll also have a solid grasp of most of the ideas that that relate to this central idea. As insane as this may sound, if we're successful, by the end of the book, we will have not only a clear picture of this very strange idea that is JP's conception of Christ but we will have also assimilated JP's conception of Christ into Christianity.

1.
ABSTRACT

Christ

What exactly is Jordan Peterson pointing at when he uses the word "Christ"? Obviously, he means something by the word, but what exactly? If you know anything about how JP thinks, you know that the answer to this question isn't going to be simple. Whatever he means by Christ, it's bound to be complex. For us, this implies that we need to unpack the meaning of the word, and unpacking what JP means by Christ isn't something that can be done in a few short sentences or even paragraphs for that matter. In fact, in order to fully unpack what JP means by Christ, we would have to reproduce most, if not all, of MoM, because in a very real sense MoM is all about Christ. MoM, however, isn't enough, not if we want to see what JP is pointing at. Like the JP in the dream from our introduction, the real JP can't actually see what he's pointing at. He is pointing at something, though, and we're interested in seeing what it is, for ourselves. So we're going to take note of the stars he's pointing at and follow the outline he's tracing. That is, we're going to examine the most significant, which is to say the defining characteristics of JP's conception of Christ, in order to produce a sort of sketch of what he is pointing at. This approach, fortunately for us, doesn't require fully unpacking JP's thinking about Christ.

Let's start by considering the idea found in this sentence fragment from MoM: "... *the pattern of action, imagination and thought that Christ represents.*" Those ten words are just packed with meaning. What we care about is that JP is telling us, in absolutely unequivocal terms, that Christ represents something. More than that, he's telling us specifically what it is that Christ represents. First and foremost, Christ represents a pattern. More specifically, Christ represents a *pattern of action, imagination, and thought.* What should be immediately obvious is that JP's conception of Christ doesn't primarily point to a person but a pattern.

This idea—that Christ represents a pattern of action, imagination, and thought—is but one characteristic or facet of JP's multifaceted conception of Christ. Here's another one. *Christ embodies the hero, grounded in tradition, who is narrative depiction of the basis for successful individual and social adaptation itself.* Once again, understanding all of the details packed into this sentence is beyond the scope of what we are doing here. For our purposes, we're only interested in specific elements within this sentence. First, as we'll see in greater detail as we progress, there's an inseparable connection between what JP means by Christ and what he means by hero. This connection is implied if not stated in the opening four words. So let's turn our attention to what JP means by hero. First, we'll note that the hero is *narrative depiction.* Like Christ, the hero is not primarily a person. The hero bears closer resemblance to a story, a story that makes visible the pattern that Christ represents. Tying these ideas together, the hero is narrative depiction of the pattern of action, imagination, and thought that renders visible *the basis for successful individual and social adaptation itself.* We could say, then, that the ideas behind the words "Christ" and "hero" have so much overlap that they are roughly interchangeable, roughly synonymous.

We've just gotten started and we've already gathered some very significant details about JP's conception of Christ. As we continue to gather these key characteristics, our sketch of JP's conception of Christ will become increasingly accurate. Along the way, we'll see how the ideas tie together, especially where we encounter words, phrases, and ideas that are, like "Christ" and "hero," roughly interchangeable. With enough of these related ideas, we'll be able to generate a clear enough sketch of what JP is pointing at, all without having to unpack all of the details.

What kind of reasoning?

This has to be said right up front: MoM is extremely difficult to quote from. Largely, this is because it is so tightly written that pulling a sentence out is like pulling at a thread in a sweater; the thread of thought that connects the sentence passes through the entire book. Everything is interconnected, and you can't fully understand the sentence without all of the associated thoughts that JP has woven together before that sentence. The effect of connecting ideas in this way is that the words and phrases that he uses most frequently are packed with meaning, meaning that can only be understood through those connected ideas. This makes it possible for him to articulate very complex ideas in relatively few words once he's developed the vocabulary, so to speak. The disadvantage, of course, is that trying to pull an isolated idea out of MoM is nearly impossible.

The way that MoM is written can be considered an example of what JP calls *reference-point reasoning* or *metonymic reasoning,* which he describes this way: *Metonymic reasoning is symbolic, in the psychoanalytic or literary sense. Metonymic means interchangeable, and more. The metonymic properties of the objects in a cognitive model mean that any or all of those objects can "stand for" any or all of the others. This capacity makes sense, since all of the objects in a given category are by definition regarded as equivalent, in some non-trivial sense... The human capacity for metaphor, aesthetic appreciation, and allusion seems integrally related to the capacity for metonymic reasoning...* You don't have to look hard to find metonymic reasoning everywhere in MoM. Here's an example: *The presumption of absolute knowledge, which is the cardinal sin of the rational spirit, is therefore prima facie equivalent to rejection of the hero—to rejection of Christ, of the Word of God, of the (divine) process that mediates between order and chaos.*

Just look at how ideas are packed one on top of another with one thing being equivalent to another and another, and so forth. In this particular example, we see that rejection of the hero is equivalent to the rejection of Christ, making whatever "hero" means equivalent, *in some non-trivial sense,* to "Christ." And both the hero and Christ are, in turn, equivalent to the Word of God, which itself is equivalent to *the (divine) process that mediates between order and chaos*. All of these "objects" are, in MoM, interchangeable in some fundamental way. Our approach won't be to unpack the meaning of each reference-point, however. Instead, we're going to explore JP's thinking in a way that resembles learning a language by immersion as we play a sort of connect-the-dots with his ideas. This should be sufficient to produce a good enough sketch of JP's conception of Christ.

Christ: A process?

Let's take another look at that last quote, the one that treats "hero" and "Christ" as equivalent:

> *The presumption of absolute knowledge, which is the cardinal sin of the rational spirit, is therefore prima facie equivalent to rejection of the hero—to rejection of Christ, of the Word of God, of the (divine) process that mediates between order and chaos.*

Christians, of course, will immediately recognize and accept the equivalence between Christ and the Word of God. That equivalence is straight from the Bible. It's doubtful, however, that any Christian would be willing to extend this equivalence to whatever JP means by the hero, and even less likely to extend it to whatever JP means by *the divine process that mediates between order and chaos*. But we aren't interested in tearing JP's ideas apart. We're interested in connecting them together. The fact that JP has connected them together is all we care about. We're interested in seeing what JP is pointing at and to do that, we need to accept his ideas as they are and see how they fit together. So if JP says that rejection of the hero, rejection of Christ, rejection of the Word of God, and rejection of the divine process that mediates between order and chaos are all equivalent in some nontrivial way, then we're simply going to add these characteristics to our sketch of his conception of Christ. Only in this way will we be able to form a clear enough image to be able to recognize what he's pointing at.

Having said that, let's consider the idea that Christ is, or is equivalent to, *the divine process that mediates between order and chaos*. We've already seen that Christ represents a *pattern of action, imagination and thought*; and now this pattern is being described as a process, and not just any process, but a process that serves a very specific function, a process that serves a particular purpose. That function, that purpose, is spelled out for us. It is to *mediate between order and chaos*.

The idea of Christ as a process is a strange idea indeed, and doubly so for anyone for whom the word "Christ" represents the person, Jesus. If this is you, then, you may be thinking that I'm taking this equivalence thing too far simply by going along with the idea that Christ represents or is equivalent to a process. Once again, however, we need to stress that we are exploring JP's conception of Christ, and on this matter he is quite clear:

> *The Old Testament offers group identity, codified by Moses, as antidote for the fallen state of man. This antidote, while useful, is incomplete—even Moses himself, a true ancestral hero, fails to reach the Promised Land. The New Testament, by contrast, offers identification with the hero as the means by which the "fallen state" and the problems of group identity might both be "permanently" transcended. The New Testament has been traditionally read as a description of a historical event, which redeemed mankind, once and for all: it might more reasonably be considered the description of a process that, if enacted, could bring about the establishment of peace on earth.*
>
> *The problem is, however, that this process cannot yet really be said to be "consciously"—that is, explicitly—understood.*
>
> – Maps of Meaning

JP's thinking, while complex, is nevertheless coherent and consistent. The ideas in MoM all fit together, and so the idea that the New Testament is a description of a process fits tightly with the idea of Christ as process.

Regardless of how we might feel about this, the ideas dovetail perfectly. And so, we will simply accept this feature as a defining characteristic of JP's Christ and move on.

Distinguishing features

Now that we have a general idea of how we are going to proceed, let's extend our net a little. There are certain ideas from MoM that find clearer expression in *12 Rules for Life* and especially in *Beyond Order*. And since these books are easier to quote from than MoM, we're going to gather some of our dots from these books as well. For instance, we've already seen how Christ represents a process. We can learn something important about this process by considering the greater context in which it fits. This context is spelled out in *Beyond Order* in this way: *We know that we are continually and inescapably playing an iterated game from which we cannot easily hide* and *Life is what repeats, and it is worth getting what repeats right.* If Life itself is an iterative game, then we should expect that this process is an iterative process. Connections like these are somewhat more difficult to identify because the connective thread is implicit rather than explicit. Nevertheless, in order to get a clear picture of this process, we must consider these less obvious but equally significant characteristics as well as the more obvious and explicit ones. Let's keep this in mind as we incorporate this idea of an iterative process into our sketch and move onto the next feature.

Abstract

There's one vital idea from MoM that applies to what we are doing here. That idea has to do with the process of abstraction itself. To see how the process of abstraction is so vitally important to JP's conception of Christ, we first need to understand its purpose. *The purpose of abstraction,* JP tells us, *is to represent experience, and to manipulate the representations, to further successful adaptation.* If these words sound familiar perhaps it's because we've already seen a strikingly similar statement describing Christ: *Christ embodies the hero, grounded in tradition, who is narrative depiction of the basis for successful individual and social adaptation itself.* Clearly, these ideas all fit together. Both speak of representing or depicting something that relates to adaptation. This isn't coincidental. In fact, with just a bit of thought, we can see that JP's conception of Christ is actually the product of this process of abstraction.

Christ and the hero constitute complex ideas, and the purpose of abstraction is to efficiently and effectively represent these ideas. That's the first half of the purpose of abstraction. The second half is that this representation allows for *playing with* the idea, or manipulating the representation in order to advance it, which is to say, clarify and sharpen the accuracy of that representation. The ideas start out rough, but like a professional gem cutter chipping away at a diamond in the rough, the ideas become clearer and clearer through this process of abstraction, assuming, of course, that the ideas are being furthered and not just distorted. The thing itself, the diamond, or in our case Christ or the hero, the pattern being represented, doesn't change so much as emerge, or come into focus and sharp contrast. That is, the representation of the thing, and not the thing itself, becomes clearer and more accurate. This evolution of the representation of something complex, like experience, takes place incrementally over time, but always moving in the direction of greater abstraction and clarity: *Each succeeding stage of abstraction modifies all others, as our ability to speak, for example, has expanded our capacity to play. As the process of abstraction continues—and information vital for survival is represented evermore simply and efficiently— what is represented transforms from the particulars of any given adaptive actions to the most general and broadly appropriate pattern of adaptation...*

What does this tell us? To start, it reinforces what we've just seen, that abstraction serves to represent information and that the process of abstraction constitutes the continued refinement and clarification of that representation. Through this process of refinement, the representation is made simpler and more efficient without the loss of any information that might be considered vital. We also see that, if we follow this process as far as it will take us, we end up with *the most general and broadly appropriate* representation of this information. This tells us something about what JP is pointing at. More specifically, it tells us that what we are looking for should constitute *an information-rich, highly abstract representation of a process expressed in its most general form.* Yes, that's a mouthful, but it's also very specific and that's a good thing, considering we're interested in forming a clear and accurate picture of JP's conception of Christ.

Real

Let's pause for a second to remind ourselves of the fact that we are operating from the assumption that JP's conception of Christ is pointing to something and, more precisely, pointing to something real. What this means is that we aren't interested in something that exists only in JP's imagination. The assumption, as we've said, is that JP's conception of Christ corresponds to something that can be found, that it is something that exists independently of JP. This assumption that it should be possible to find what JP is pointing at is critically important. So, let's see if we can justify this assumption. Once again, we're going to allow JP to guide our thinking, but we're going to take a minor step back from MoM to focus not on the content of the book but rather on the approach JP used in writing MoM. Here's how JP describes his approach to Sam Harris:

> *In MoM, I tried to do what E. O. Wilson recommended, but this was before he wrote his book. I tried to use a consilience approach. So I looked at [1] multiple religious systems, I looked at [2] Christianity, I looked at [3] evolutionary biology, I looked at [4] philosophy, I looked at [5] neuroscience and I looked at [6] the literature on emotion and motivation and the literature on play, that was very nicely delineated by Piaget and I tried to see where there was a pattern that repeated across all the dimensions of evaluation, which is exactly what you do, for example when you use your five senses to detect something real in the world, and that's what Wilson recommended was a consilience approach.*

And so, my proposition was, if it manifests itself here [1] and here
[2], and here [3], and here [4], and here [5], and here [6], six
places, and it's always the same pattern, then the probability that
that pattern exists, independent of my "delusional interpretation,"
is radically decreased.[3]

The first thing that we should note about JP's consilience approach is that its purpose was to ensure that his thinking remained grounded in reality. The second thing to note is that JP himself is making the assertion that he's looking for a pattern that exists independent of his thinking. In essence, then, what we are doing is simply following in his footsteps, looking for this pattern that exists independently, which exists in reality. JP's approach was meant to converge on something, something real, and so we can proceed with a modicum of assurance that we are justified in our assumption.

Creative: Generates beauty

The creative capacity is divine Logos, which in the course of its
development necessitates recognition of the inevitability of fail-
ure and death. That is in part the meaning of the symbol of the
Christian crucifixion, which paradoxically melds mortality with
divinity—which is representative of the "mortal god," infinitely
creative, responsible, and vulnerable.

– Maps of Meaning

The divine Logos is equivalent or interchangeable with the Word of God, which in turn is interchangeable with Christ. So here we are given another equivalence to Christ, one more thing that Christ represents. So let's add *creative capacity* to our list of defining characteristics of JP's conception of Christ, and turn our attention to another idea that JP connects to the divine Logos. The connection is made in *Beyond Order* where JP is discussing art

---

3   Sam Harris & Jordan Peterson in Vancouver, Part 1: https://youtu.be/jey_CzIOfYE?t=6103
     Also, it should be noted that JP accidentally says "decreased" where he obviously meant
     "increased."

and the role that it plays. Within that discussion, JP quotes a well-known verse from Matthew, but he takes the liberty of modifying the verse in such a way that it reveals another of these connecting ideas. Here is how he puts it: *As it is said, Man shall not live by bread alone" (Matthew 4:4). That is exactly right. We live by beauty. We live by literature. We live by art.*

To see the equivalence being made in this quote, we have to know how the verse he is quoting actually ends. "Man shall not live by bread alone, but by every word that proceeds from the mouth of God." While it's possible that he's misrepresenting Scripture, what's more likely is that he sees *beauty, literature, and art* as interchangeable with the divine Logos. And so, whether or not we agree with this equivalence between beauty and the divine Logos, we can agree that it's part of JP's conception of Christ.

> *Beauty leads you back to what you have lost. Beauty reminds you of what remains forever immune to cynicism. Beauty beckons in a manner that straightens your aim. Beauty reminds you that there is lesser and greater value.*

It's fitting, I suppose, that JP's conception of Christ should include beauty as one of its defining characteristics. Any pattern of action, imagination, and thought that is not also attractive would not motivate imitation. And so we can add this characteristic to our list as well.

Process

Let's return to a quote we quickly examined earlier, but this time we'll continue reading:

> *Christ embodies the hero, grounded in tradition, who is narrative depiction of the basis for successful individual and social adaptation itself. As the Word, "made flesh" (John 1:14) there "in the beginning" (John 1:1), he represents, simultaneously, the power that divides order from chaos, and tradition rendered spiritual, abstract, declarative, semantic. His manner of being is that which*

moves morality itself from rule of law to rule of spirit, which means process. Spirit is process, simultaneously opposed to and responsible for generating static being.

Our interest in this quote arises from the fact that it contains another direct statement of what Christ represents. These direct references to what Christ represents are to us JP's finger pointing directly at the most relevant characteristics of his conception of Christ, so let's take note of what he's pointing at. Here Christ represents two things, simultaneously. First Christ represents *the power that divides order from chaos.* We've already seen a variation of this when we saw that Christ is *the process that mediates between order and chaos,* and so this quote underscores the significance of this characteristic. Secondly, Christ also represents *tradition rendered spiritual.* And for clarity concerning the meaning of spiritual, we need only look a little further to see, first that *Spirit is process* and secondly that Spirit is *simultaneously opposed to and responsible for generating static being.*

Let's look at another informative quote that reveals another connection to Christ:

We use stories to regulate our emotions and govern our behavior; use stories to provide the present we inhabit with a determinate point of reference—the desired future. The optimal "desired future" is not a state, however, but a process—the (intrinsically compelling) process of mediating between order and chaos; the process of the incarnation of Logos—the word—which is the world-creating principle.

– Maps of Meaning

Here we have an only slightly less direct statement of what Christ represents. We know that Christ represents *the process that mediates between order and chaos* and that Christ is *narrative depiction,* and so this reference to stories shouldn't throw us off. By providing *the present we inhabit with a determinate point of reference,* stories orient us by pointing towards the *desired future.* And here's where things get interesting. The very best possible future, the optimal desired future, also happens to be a process— and wouldn't you know it, that process is the process that mediates between order and chaos or Christ. But let's not stop at that, because JP sheds further light on this process when he elaborates by telling us that this process is the process of *incarnating the Logos*, which is *the world creating principle*. These ideas, of course, dovetail nicely with the idea that the New Testament is a description of a process *that, if enacted, could bring about the establishment of peace on earth.*

Process is the thread that connects these ideas. Notice that *Spirit is process*, that the *incarnation of Logos* is process, and that *the optimal desired future* is also processes. Next, notice that implicit in this process is the act of discrimination, the act of differentiating between or *mediating between order and chaos*. We see, from the numerous repetitions of this idea of mediating between order and chaos, just how vital the idea is to JP's conception of Christ. The centrality of this one characteristic cannot be overstated. So let's look at one final quote from MoM that ties these ideas together. Recalling that *Christ embodies the hero,* we see these ideas summed up in, *The hero is, after all, incarnation of the process by which chaos is transformed into order.* All of this, of course, is simply to say that whatever we find that matches JP's conception of Christ absolutely must *embody* this process of mediating between order and chaos.

Spoiler alert

Let's return to the dream that opened the introduction for a moment. Let's imagine ourselves back in that dream staring into the triangle that JP has outlined. As we gaze into the defined area, we begin to see a form emerging. But, at that moment the dream takes an abrupt and unexpected turn and the scene changes. We're still in the field, still observing JP, and he's still pointing, only it's no longer nighttime but mid-day, and he's no longer pointing into the sky. Instead, he's holding a bow. We observe that he's drawn the bow-string all the way back and we intuit that he's about to let the arrow fly. We're curious about what he's aiming at, so we take careful note of the direction he's facing and the angle at which he is holding the bow. Our eye traces the trajectory we believe the arrow will follow and we see, in the distance, what we are certain must be his intended target.

What we've been doing so far is gathering information about JP's conception of Christ in order to form an impression of where he is aiming. Having gathered the information, it's time to trace out the trajectory of his arrow. Of course, at this point, the analogy breaks down. It isn't very likely, perhaps even impossible, that anyone would be able to form a clear mental image of JP's conception of Christ from the features we've gathered together. What's more, I don't want to give the impression that I used such a methodical approach in discovering what JP is pointing at.

In reality, what happened is that I spent an inordinate amount of time, over a period of about a year, immersed in MoM and through this prolonged exercise I became very familiar with JP's ideas. Immediately on the heels of this exercise, I stumbled onto something that bore a remarkable similarity to this process that mediates between order and chaos. So we're not even going to try to pretend that it's possible to trace the trajectory of the arrow. Instead, I'm simply going to reveal what JP is pointing at, the intended target, and then we'll look at how it shares all of the same key features. That is, we'll examine how it maps perfectly to JP's conception of Christ.

In case you would like the chance to discover it for yourself, I would like to give you the opportunity to do just that before revealing the answer. So, if you want to give it a shot, get your hands on a copy of James Gleick's *Chaos: Making a New Science*. In that book, you'll find a description of a process that matches JP's description of this process that mediates between order and chaos.

Before unveiling what JP's conception of Christ is pointing at, it's worth noting how appropriate it is that it would be found within the greater context of this particular book, a book about the science of chaos. Chaos, of course, is the thread that connects the two books. JP uses the word no less than 250 times in MoM. What's more, there's a lot of overlap between the behavior of chaotic systems, the centerpiece of Gleick's book, and the behavior of the more mythological chaos that JP focuses on. More importantly, however, Gleick's *Chaos* is a story about a revolutionary update in the domain of physics, and if you're familiar with JP's ideas, you'll know how significant revolutionary updates are in his thinking. As we shall see, there really couldn't be a more fitting place to find a description of a process that mediates between order and chaos.

> *It is therefore simplest to assume that all there is of reality is experience, in being and progressive unfolding.*
>
> – Maps of Meaning

> *To some physicists chaos is a science of process rather than state, of becoming rather than being.*
>
> – James Gleick, *Chaos: Making a New Science*

JP's Christ unveiled

Now that you've had the opportunity to discover what JP's conception of Christ is pointing at, for yourself, it's time to pull the curtains back, reach into the shadows, and draw it out into the open for all to see. If you read Gleick's *Chaos* in order to make the discovery yourself, I hope the answer jumped out at you when you got to the section on the Mandelbrot set. If it did jump out at you, then I trust that you also made a clear distinction between the Mandelbrot set and the process that produces the Mandelbrot. This distinction between the process and the thing produced by the process is critical. Recall that *Spirit is process, simultaneously opposed to and responsible for generating static being*. Well, the Mandelbrot set itself constitutes the product of the process, the *static being* that is brought into existence, or at the very least, made visible by the process. To be perfectly clear, then, JP's conception of Christ points to the process that produces the Mandelbrot set.

Christ's life and words—as archetypal exemplars of the heroic manner of being—place explicit stress on the process of life, rather than upon its products.

– Maps of Meaning

Even if you're familiar with the Mandelbrot set, it's very likely that you've never given much thought to the process that produces it. Let's try to make up for that. First, a bit of context is in order. The process that produces the Mandelbrot set emerged as part of a larger evolution in mathematics. More specifically, this process was part of a more general discovery, the discovery of a new type of geometry. Understanding how this new type of geometry differs from the old is a critical piece of the puzzle, so let's look at how Gleick describes how a handful of mathematicians changed the rules about how to make geometrical shapes.

Julia, Fatou, Hubbard, Barnsley, Mandelbrot—these mathematicians changed the rules about how to make geometrical shapes. The Euclidean and Cartesian methods of turning equations into curves are familiar to anyone who has studied high school geometry or found a point on a map using two coordinates. Standard geometry takes an equation and asks for the set of numbers that satisfy it. The solutions to an equation like $x^2 + y^2 = 1$, then, form a shape, in this case a circle. Other simple equations produce other pictures, the ellipses, parabolas, and hyperbolas of conic sections or even the more complicated shapes produced by differential equations in phase space. But when a geometer iterates an equation instead of solving it, the equation becomes a process instead of a description, dynamic instead of static. When a number goes into the equation, a new number comes out; the new number goes in, and so on, points hopping from place to place. A point is plotted not when it satisfies the equation but when it produces a certain kind of behavior. One behavior might be a steady state. Another *might be a convergence to a periodic repetition of states. Another might be an out-of-control race to infinity.*

Notice that this new geometry *iterates an equation instead of solving it,* and thereby transforms the equation into a *process instead of a description, dynamic instead of static.* Can you hear the echo of JP's ideas in these words? Even the very language being used is the same. But let's make sure that the similarities here are more than superficial.

Let's start by looking at the process itself. The first thing we want to note is that this process is an iterative process. That, in itself, is significant because, we've seen that *We know that we are continually and inescapably playing an iterated game from which we cannot easily hide,* and *Life is what repeats, and it is worth getting what repeats right.* More importantly, though, we need to understand the iterative nature of this process in order to see how it *mediates between order and chaos.* So, let's look again at the foregoing quote where JG states: *When a number goes into the equation, a new number comes out; the new number goes in, and so on, points hopping from place to place. A point is plotted not when it satisfies the equation but when it produces a certain kind of behavior.* I hope that from this description you can see that Gleick is describing a feedback loop, a feedback process. You perform a calculation and the output of the calculation is used as the next input to the same calculation, and so on, the output feeding back into the process as its input in a fashion reminiscent of JP's *uroboros, the self-consuming serpent.*

We should also note that the calculation itself never changes. It's the same calculation being repeated over and over, each point being treated exactly the same. It's a very simple process as Gleick makes clear: *... the calculation was simple, because the process itself was so simple: the iteration in the complex plane of the mapping $z \to z^2 + c$. Take a number, multiply it by itself, and add the original number.* This act of performing, or iterating, this calculation produces a new point after each iteration, and if you were to plot the result of each calculation, you would see *points hopping from place to place.*

This hopping around constitutes the behavior of the point under iteration. You pick a point start iterating it through the equation and observe its behavior. *A point is plotted not when it satisfies the equation but when it produces a certain kind of behavior.* In the case of the process that produces the Mandelbrot set, the observed behaviors are grouped into two distinct categories, which serve to differentiate between those points that are in the set and those that aren't: *To test a point, take the complex number; square it; add the original number; square the result; add the original number; square the result—and so on, over and over again. If the total runs away to infinity, then the point is not in the Mandelbrot set. If the total remains finite (it could be trapped in some repeating loop, or it could wander chaotically), then the point is in the Mandelbrot set.*

For any given point, this process produces one of two distinct types of behavior. Either the calculation will *run off to infinity* or it will *remain finite*. Those points that demonstrate the *off to infinity* behavior are excluded from the set. The other points—those that don't run off to infinity but remain finite—belong to the set.

Orbits

The Mandelbrot set is a collection of points. Every point in the complex plane—that is, every complex number—is either in the set or outside it. One way to define the set is in terms of a test for every point, involving some simple iterated arithmetic.

– Chaos

We've been talking about the behavior of points under iteration of this function. Now that we're familiar with the two basic categories of behavior that a point under iteration will demonstrate, we should note that there is a name for this idea of *behavior under iteration.* Mathematicians call it the point's orbit. More than that, both types of orbits also have names. An orbit that demonstrates the *off to infinity* behavior is called unstable, while the other is called stable. Armed with this terminology, we can say that points that demonstrate an unstable orbit do not belong to the set. Only those points that demonstrate a stable orbit are in the set.[4]

While the orbits that these points trace out are nothing like the orbit of the earth around the sun, the idea lends itself to making an important point. Life on earth depends on the fact that the earth's orbit around the sun has remained stable over a very long period of time. If the earth's orbit were to become unstable, for whatever reason, and the earth flew off out of the solar system—heading off essentially to infinity—we all know what that would spell: chaos. So we see that stable/unstable, order/chaos, these pairs of ideas, are interchangeable. I trust you see where this is headed. The process that produces the Mandelbrot set discriminates between stable and unstable orbits, which is to say it discriminates and sorts between order and chaos. So this process literally mediates between order and chaos. And what we see is that JP couldn't have pointed more clearly at this target if he tried.

It's worth emphasizing the way in which this process differentiates between points and splits, or divides the entire complex plane into two and only two categories of mutually incompatible behavior. In order to appreciate the significance of this, we need to recognize it as the most general form or representation of JP's mythological *hostile brothers,* which represent the *archetypes of response to the unknown* in MoM. These brothers illustrate two mutually incompatible ways of facing the unknown, with one brother, the *mythological hero* who *faces the unknown with the presumption of its benevolence,* while the other, the *eternal adversary shrinks from contact with everything he does not understand.* This shrinking is a *moving away from* in a manner illustrated by the unstable orbits that *fly away from.* This process, then, serves to illustrate or perhaps make visible the two *attractors* that exert influence on the *individual.* That is, this process allows us to visualize, at a very abstract and general level, two transpersonal patterns of behavior and

---

4   There are numerous websites that allow you to explore these orbits yourself, and I strongly recommend that you do so. I recommend the site https://www.geogebra.org/m/ tEetDqXF, which not only plots the orbits of the point (c) as you move it around in the complex plane but also provides the numerical results of each iteration.

schemas of representation, comprising the individual as such, embodied in mythology as the hostile brothers. These two *transpersonal patterns of behavior* act as two competing attracting forces vying for control over the individual's behavior in a manner similar to the attractors in the Mandelbrot set: *The boundary is where points are slowest to escape the pull of the set. It is as if they are balanced between competing attractors, one at zero and the other, in effect, ringing the set at a distance of infinity.*

Exploration

Each succeeding stage of abstraction modifies all others, as our ability to speak, for example, has expanded our capacity to play. As the process of abstraction continues—and information vital for survival is represented evermore simply and efficiently—what is represented transforms from the particulars of any given adaptive actions to the most general and broadly appropriate pattern of adaptation—that of creative exploration itself.

– Maps of Meaning

Earlier, when we looked at this quote, we omitted the ending, the final five words. We did so purposefully because those words at the end of that particular sentence constitute the one place where JP points us in the wrong direction. Following his train of thought, we see that JP has concluded that Christ, in the final analysis, in its most abstracted and generalized form, boils down to *creative exploration itself*. To JP, therefore, this is not another facet or characteristic of Christ but the thing itself. This is JP's own answer to the question of where the arrow will strike, as it were.

What JP fails to realize, however, is that he has taken his ideas a step too far. Even packed with all of the meaning that he's packed into those three words, *creative exploration itself*, he's nevertheless lost all the *information vital for survival*. He's whittled it down to something so general that it carries no vital information at all. Having said that, however, we still want to examine how this idea of *creative exploration itself* fits into the picture. This remains, after all, another equivalence to Christ, and we don't want to ignore one that is obviously so significant to JP that he mistakes it for the actual thing. So, at the very least, we need to ensure that this element is captured or represented by this *process that mediates between order and chaos*. Fortunately, Gleick doesn't leave us guessing about this: *Unlike the traditional shapes of geometry, circles and ellipses and parabolas, the Mandelbrot set allows no shortcuts. The only way to see what kind of shape goes with a particular equation is by trial and error, and the trial-and-error style brought the explorers of this new terrain closer in spirit to Magellan than to Euclid.*

Because of the sheer number of calculations needed to produce the Mandelbrot set, the process is always automated. That makes it easy to forget about the fact that the process must test each and every point, observe its behavior and use that behavior to discriminate between those points that remain in a stable orbit and those that fly away. But just because we forget about this doesn't change the fact that *the Mandelbrot set allows no shortcuts*. There is no way to tell how any given point will behave under iteration other than to test or explore its behavior by iterating it through this process. And so Gleick likens these mathematicians to explorers charting new terrain, explorers in *spirit to Magellan*. So we see that exploration, perhaps even *creative exploration itself*, is built right into the process. So even here we see evidence that JP is pointing us in the right direction only, his arrow has overshot the target by a fraction.

Yes, but Real?

Recall how we took the time to examine the *consilience approach* that JP took in writing MoM, and how we noted that this approach should point to something real. This raises the immediate question of whether or not this process constitutes something real. Let's see if we can answer this question by turning to something most everyone will consider real, a bar of iron. Let's imagine we have a bar of iron and that half the bar is magnetized and the other half isn't. We know that the atoms that make up the side that's magnetized all point (magnetically) in the same direction. Obviously, what this means is that the way in which these atoms are arranged is orderly. More precisely, the atoms are all *oriented in the world*, the physical world, such that they all point in the same direction. The atoms in the other end of the bar, the non-magnetized end, all point in random directions. That is, the direction these atoms point in is characterized by disorder, or chaos.

Now, in a bar of iron where one end is magnetized and the other isn't, there will be a boundary that separates the magnetized side from the non-magnetized side. This boundary, then, literally, physically constitutes the boundary between order and disorder, between order and chaos. This is about as physically real as things get, wouldn't you agree? Now consider the following with respect to this boundary:

> *Fractal basin boundaries addressed deep issues in theoretical physics. Phase transitions were matters of thresholds, and Peitgen and Richter looked at one of the best-studied kinds of phase transitions, magnetization and nonmagnetization in materials. Their pictures of such boundaries displayed the peculiarly beautiful complexity that was coming to seem so natural, cauliflower shapes with progressively more tangled knobs and furrows. As they varied the parameters and increased their magnification of details, one picture seemed more and more random, until suddenly, unexpectedly, deep in the heart of a bewildering region, appeared a familiar oblate form, studded with buds: the Mandelbrot set, every tendril and every atom in place. It was another signpost of universality. "Perhaps we should believe in magic," they wrote.*
>
> *– Chaos*

Here we find the Mandelbrot set appearing in reality, and precisely where we would expect to find it, at the border between order and chaos. It only stands to reason that if the Mandelbrot set is there, then the process that produces it must also be there as well, somehow. And so, unlike JP's *creative exploration itself*, we can boldly state that what we've found exists, actually exists, independently in reality. What this means is that JP's consilience approach did in fact point to something in reality and, even though JP couldn't see what that something was, he did a remarkable job of pointing straight at it.

Eternal

Having firmly established that the process that generates the Mandelbrot set constitutes the process that mediates between order and chaos, it's worth noting that both Peterson and Gleick, point, in their own way, to the eternal nature of this process which is JP's conception of Christ.

> Sometimes "adaptation" is merely a matter of the adjustment of the means to an end. More rarely, but equally necessarily, adaptation is reconceptualization of "what is known" (unbearable present, desirable future and means to attain such)—because what is known is out of date, and therefore deadly. It is the sum of these processes that manifests itself in the Judeo-Christian tradition as the mythic Word of God (and which is embodied in Christ, the Christian culture-hero). This is the force that generates subject and object from the primordial chaos (and, therefore, which predates the existence of both); the force that engenders the tradition that makes vulnerable existence possible, in the face of constant mortal threat; and the force that updates protective tradition, when it has become untenable, and tyrannical, on account of its age.

– Maps of Meaning

We've seen enough of these interchangeable ideas by now that we can recognize the fact that *the force that generates subject and object from primordial chaos* is equivalent to *the process that mediates between order and chaos*, or Christ. This is the force that generates subject and object, order, from the primordial chaos. The use of the word "primordial" in this instance points all the way back to Big Bang, before anything had form. And this force *predates* both *subject and object*, making this force essentially eternal in nature. Now consider what Gleick says about the Mandelbrot set, and, by implication the process that generates it:

The Mandelbrot set, in the same way, exists. It existed before Peitgen and Richter began turning it into an art form, before Hubbard and Douady understood its mathematical essence, even before Mandelbrot discovered it. It existed as soon as science created a context—a framework of complex numbers and a notion of iterated functions. Then it waited to be unveiled. Or perhaps it existed even earlier, as soon as nature began organizing itself by means of simple physical laws, repeated with infinite patience and everywhere the same.

– Chaos

Infinitely creative, etc...

I strongly suspect that a thorough and detailed analysis of the ways in which the ideas in Gleick's *Chaos* converge with the ideas in MoM and especially JP's conception of Christ would require volumes. We've really only skimmed the surface in our exploration of these similarities. Nevertheless, the similarities that we've highlighted make a compelling enough case on their own.

It remains that JP's conception of Christ points at something. For JP, that something is *creative exploration itself,* but as we've just seen, the process of abstraction should have led to something that is not only highly abstracted and very general, like *creative exploration itself,* but it should have done so without the loss of vital information. That is, it should have led to something that is also *information-rich* as a result of the process of abstraction, which distills and condenses the *information vital for survival.* You're free, of course, to accept JP's *creative exploration itself* as the thing that his conception of Christ points to, but that would mean accepting a solution where the information has been boiled off rather than merely *represented evermore simply and efficiently.* By contrast, what we've discovered not only matches numerous key characteristics of JP's description of Christ, and in very specific and precise ways, but it is also packed with information. Just consider what this simple process produces:

THE MANDELBROT SET IS the most complex object in mathematics, its admirers like to say. An eternity would not be enough time to see it all, its disks studded with prickly thorns, its spirals and filaments curling outward and around, bearing bulbous molecules that hang, infinitely variegated, like grapes on God's personal vine. Examined in color through the adjustable window of a computer screen, the Mandelbrot set seems more fractal than fractals, so rich is its complication across scales. A cataloguing of the different images within it or a numerical description of the set's outline would require an infinity of information. But here is a paradox: to send a full description of the set over a transmission line requires just a few dozen characters of code. A terse computer program contains enough information to reproduce the entire set. Those who were first to understand the way the set commingles complexity and simplicity were caught unprepared— even Mandelbrot. The Mandelbrot set became a kind of public emblem for chaos, appearing on the glossy covers of conference brochures and engineering quarterlies, forming the centerpiece of an exhibit of computer art that traveled internationally in 1985 and 1986. Its beauty was easy to feel from these pictures; harder to grasp was the meaning it had for the mathematicians who slowly understood it.

– Chaos

We've stated, rather emphatically, that JP's conception of Christ points to this process that produces the most complex object in mathematics. While this is entirely true, it isn't the entire truth. What I mean by that is that we've been essentially ignoring half of JP's conception of Christ. JP's conception of Christ spans more than one level of analysis. For clarity's sake, we've constrained our focus almost exclusively to what might be considered the most fundamental level of analysis. Put another way, we've spent this chapter exploring the foundation while ignoring the edifice that rests on that foundation. This approach of focusing on the most fundamental level of analysis has paid off, because it has allowed us to follow the process of abstraction all the way to the *most general and broadly appropriate pattern* that matches JP's conception of Christ. And now that we're clear about the foundation, we're prepared to shift our attention to a completely different level of analysis, one that comes much closer to where we live our everyday lives.

Leveling up

To help us make the leap to the next level of analysis, we're going to tie together an idea that is present in MoM but comes across a lot clearer in *Chaos*. The connection has to do with this idea of different levels of analysis. To see the connection, let's reconsider a quote we saw earlier, where JP tells us that Christ *represents, simultaneously, the power that divides order from chaos, and tradition rendered spiritual.* In these words, we catch a glimpse of the two levels of analysis that we are primarily concerned with. The *power that divides order from chaos* concerns the most fundamental level of analysis while *tradition rendered spiritual* belongs to a different level of analysis. The former is more abstract, more general in nature, encompassing all of order and chaos. This level reaches down into the interaction of fundamental elements of matter as we saw at the boundary between magnetized and non-magnetized materials. The latter is more specific, clearly operating at a different level, at the level of human interaction, at the level of human culture. This level is concerned with human dynamics.

Jumping from the more fundamental level of analysis to the level that concerns human interactions isn't a simple matter, however. We want to make sure that the edifice rests squarely on the foundation and is secured to it, as it were. To do that we're going to consider the nature of the Mandelbrot set because it affords us a way of jumping up a level of analysis without losing touch with the lower level.

The Mandelbrot set is a fractal structure. It is the archetypal represen-tation of what fractal means. Benoit Mandelbrot explored all sorts of things that, on the surface, should have nothing in common with each other, things like the price of cotton over time, and noise in electronic communications, and the pattern of river floods. And yet, there was something that these things shared in common.

> Mandelbrot's other advantage was the picture of reality he had begun forming in his encounters with cotton prices, with electronic transmission noise, and with river floods. The picture was beginning to come into focus now. His studies of irregular patterns in natural processes and his exploration of infinitely complex shapes had an intellectual intersection: a quality of self-similarity. Above all, fractal meant self-similar.

> Self-similarity is symmetry across scale. It implies recursion, pattern inside of pattern.

If you're familiar with MoM, this pattern inside of pattern or symmetry across scale features prominently, only using slightly different vocabulary. In MoM, you have *nested* elements such as stories, nested groups and individuals, and nested structures. In fact, in MoM, JP tells us that *Reality is made up of nested interpretations.* This is how JP spans across scale, by relying on self-similarity. We caught a glimpse of this idea in JP's consilience approach where he clearly states that he's looking at a *pattern that repeated across all the dimensions of evaluation.* He never uses the word "self-similarity" but he was clearly guided by the same thing that guided Benoit Mandelbrot, self-similarity, symmetry across scale. Self-similarity, then, will serve as our guide as well, as we jump from the most fundamental level of analysis up to the scale of human interactions, of human dynamics.

> It is possible for two phenomena to be different, at one level of analysis, and similar at another.

> – Maps of Meaning

2.

EXPLICITLY UNDERSTOOD

Now what?

JP's conception of Christ points to—or perhaps more accurately maps to—the process that reveals the Mandelbrot set. As true as this is, it nevertheless falls far short of capturing a complete representation of Christ as JP has conceived. We've certainly found something very abstract that matches JP's conception of Christ, but what we've found is so abstract that we cannot immediately see how it relates to morality. That is, we seem to have lost all connection to anything remotely approaching something that most of us might even possibly associate with Christ. In the previous chapter, we hinted that this disconnect might have something to do with the level of analysis or scale we were forced to concentrate on in order to bring *the most general and broadly appropriate* representation of the pattern that Christ represents into sharp focus. Having found that most abstract and general representation of this pattern at the most fundamental level of analysis, it's time to shift our attention to a different scale, to switch levels of analysis to the level that includes human behavior. Stating this another way, having laid the foundation, we are now ready to build on it.

We've now moved beyond what JP can see, which places us in uncharted territory. Fortunately, having discovered the archetypal form underpinning JP's conceptions of Christ, we can now use it to guide our steps. More precisely, owing to the fact that the process that produces the Mandelbrot set produces a structure that is fractal, we have the advantage of knowing that

JP's conception of Christ should demonstrate symmetry across scale. Without this knowledge, this understanding of what self-similarity implies, switching scales would leave us without a starting point and with nothing to guide us in our search. But armed with this understanding, we have a powerful tool at our disposal for ensuring that we stay on course.

Also, now that we understand that JP's conception of Christ spans across scales, we can continue to use JP's conception of Christ to guide us by focusing on those aspects of his conception of Christ that manifest at the scale of human interaction. So, despite finding ourselves in uncharted territory, we are not without a solid foundation and clear direction. And with that, let's switch our level of analysis.

One piece short

JP has done all of this work in delineating precisely what Christ represents. He's done so out of a sort of compulsion. We're given a glimpse into this aspect of JP's journey in MoM, where he includes a letter to his father from which following paragraph is taken:

> I don't completely understand the driving force behind what I have been working on, although I understand it better now than I used to, three or four years ago, when it was literally driving me crazy. I had been obsessed with the idea of war for three or four years prior to that, often dreaming extremely violent dreams, centered around the theme of destruction. I believe now that my concern with death on a mass scale was intimately tied into my personal life, and that concerns with the meaning of life on a personal level (which arise with the contemplation of death) took a general form for me, which had to do with the value of humanity, and the purpose of life in general.

There was a driving force motivating JP's search for Christ. He didn't do it just for fun. He was contending with a problem, a serious problem, the problem of war. By "contending with," I mean he was earnestly trying to understand the problem, not just for the sake of understanding it but with an eye on solving the problem. He writes to his father, *I came to believe that survival itself, and more, depended upon a solution to the problem of war.* And within this letter to his father, we are also given a fairly clear picture of JP's perspective on the Bible:

> *Mythological renditions of history, like those in the Bible, are just as "true" as the standard Western empirical renditions, just as literally true, but how they are true is different. Western historians describe (or think they describe) "what" happened. The traditions of mythology and religion describe the significance of what happened (and it must be noted that if what happens is without significance, it is irrelevant).*

What immediately follows this letter to his father is revealing:

> *It has been almost fifteen years since I first grasped the essence of the paradox that lies at the bottom of human motivation for evil: People need their group identification, because that identification protects them, literally, from the terrible forces of the unknown. It is for this reason that every individual who is not decadent will strive to protect his territory, actual and psychological. But the tendency to protect means hatred of the other, and the inevitability of war—and we are now too technologically powerful to engage in war. To allow the other victory, however—or even continued existence, on his term—means subjugation, dissolution of protective structure, and exposure to that which is most feared. For me, this meant "damned if you do, damned if you don't": belief systems regulate affect, but conflict between belief systems is inevitable.*

> *Formulation and understanding of this terrible paradox devastated me. I had always been convinced that sufficient understanding of a problem—any problem—would lead to its resolution. Here I was, however—possessed of understanding that seemed*

not only sufficient but complete—caught nonetheless between the devil and the deep blue sea.

We see, then, that JP had been trying to resolve the problem of war and he'd made tremendous progress, to the point of understanding the problem not only sufficiently but completely. Nevertheless, even with a complete understanding of the problem, JP is left without a solution, unless of course you accept *creative exploration itself* as the solution. But we've already seen how this solution is too general. He's essentially run into the problem he describes to SH as the death of God. *The problem with extracting out the highest god from the panoply of gods is the ideal becomes so abstract that it disappears. That's the death of God.*[5] So what we see is that JP has followed this process of abstraction in search of a solution to the problem of war only to come up with a solution so abstract and general that it has evaporated, and to some degree, JP is aware of this.

We seem to have reached an impasse. JP himself has taken his own thinking as far as it could go, or so it seems. There is, however, a train of thought that JP begins but abandons, which can serve as our starting point. This undeveloped train of thought starts with the observation that *The New Testament has been traditionally read as a description of a historical event, which redeemed mankind, once and for all; it might more reasonably be considered the description of a process that, if enacted, could bring about the establishment of peace on earth.* Here we see that JP knows where the solution lies. But instead of following this particular train of thought, he abruptly brings it to a halt with these words: *The problem is, however, that this process cannot yet really be said to be "consciously"—that is, explicitly—understood.* With that, JP abandons this train of thought and, as a result, provides us with an opportunity to explore a possibility that he seems to have written off as impossible, that of consciously or explicitly understanding the process that the New Testament is a description of.

---

5   Sam Harris, Jordan Peterson & Douglas Murray in Dublin, Part 3. https://youtube/
     PqpYxD71hJU?t=3785

Turning to an analogy to clarify what we are saying here, we can think of JP as working on a puzzle. He's got all the pieces on the table and he's arranged them so that they all fit together. Unfortunately, JP is missing a piece of the puzzle, a critical piece. It's clear that he knows about the missing piece because he tells us precisely what it is, an explicit understanding of the process the New Testament is a description of.

This brings us to something I alluded to in the introduction. In becoming familiar with JP's ideas while at the same time trying to *get my story straight*, I discovered something remarkable. While I didn't spell it out in the introduction, when I considered each of the chapters in my life and attempted to line everything up into a single narrative, what I discovered was that my life followed the pattern of the hero myth that JP lays out in detail in MoM. Even more remarkable, the particular pattern that my life traced out appeared to match the pattern of what JP would call a *cultural* revolutionary hero. We'll look at the significance of the word "cultural" shortly, but for now, let's review the pattern that my life's story traces out.

My journey or story consists of three distinct chapters, each covering a period of approximately twenty years. The first chapter was spent immersed in the Roman Catholic culture of my parents. It consisted, primarily of the cyclical repetition of rituals and ceremonies, which were reinforced by an abundance of imagistic representations of various aspects of the Catholic faith. In the next chapter, I walked away from my Catholic roots to become a fundamentalist evangelical Protestant Christian. Really, however, all these terms really mean is that I spent the next twenty years as an apprentice or disciple of Christ. The story really only gets interesting in the final chapter, which starts with me walking away from my religious worldview altogether. And this act of jettisoning my religious worldview constituted diving head-long into what JP calls the *nihilistic void*. After spending years sinking to the bottom of that seemingly bottomless abyss, I experienced something like what JP would call the discovery of my dead father, in the belly of that beast. That was in 2012, and since then I've been slowly dragging this back to the surface as it were. And, as it turns out, this thing just happens to be the missing piece to JP's puzzle.

The nature of the problem

Before revealing this missing piece of the puzzle, we're going to want to make sure that we understand the nature of the problem that JP has been contending with. Our reasoning here is simple. Unless we understand the problem, we're unlikely to even recognize that the problem exists, much less recognize the necessity of solving it. If we don't realize what we stand to lose by leaving the problem unaddressed, we won't even care about whether or not the problem is ever solved. On that note, let's take a step back and examine the problem itself.

> *Every culture maintains certain key beliefs, which are centrally important to that culture, upon which all secondary beliefs are predicated. These key beliefs cannot be easily given up, because if they are, everything falls, and the unknown once again rules. Western morality, western behavior, is for example predicated on the assumption that every individual is sacred. This belief was already extant in its nascent form, among the ancient Egyptians, and provides the very cornerstone of Judeo-Christian civilization.*

> *Successful challenge to this idea would invalidate the actions and goals of the western individual, would destroy the western dominance hierarchy—the social context for individual action. In the absence of this central assumption, the body of western law—formalized myth, codified morality—erodes and falls. There are no individual rights, no individual value—and the foundation of the western social (and psychological) structure dissolves. The Second World and Cold wars were fought largely to eliminate such a challenge.*

Here JP tells us that the foundation of Judeo-Christian civilization consists of a key belief, the belief in the *sacredness of the individual*. This idea, this belief, constitutes the very foundation of Western culture. As with any structure, if you destroy the foundation, the structure itself will inevitably eventually collapse. This is where things get ugly. You see, this belief is communicated and kept alive by the culture's central myth. What this means is that if you destroy the myth you not only challenge but actually destroy the very basis for the belief. And this is where the true nature of the problem jumps out, because, as JP informs us, *The great forces of empiricism and rationality and the great technique of the experiment have killed myth, and it cannot be resurrected—or so it seems.*

The problem that JP is contending with is this. The foundation of Western culture lies in its key belief which has its basis in the culture's central myth but myth itself has been killed and cannot be resurrected. The implication is clear though perhaps so frightening that few are willing to face it. Stated simply, Western culture has demolished its own foundation. This has already taken place. And so Western culture currently stands in a similar condition to that of the Twin Towers after being struck by the terrorist-hijacked airliners. Just as each crash guaranteed the inevitable collapse, destruction of our central myth, or myth itself guarantees the collapse of Western culture. And just like the New York residents who witnessed the crash that fated these towers to collapse, we fail to acknowledge the possibility of cultural collapse much less realize its imminence. But JP sees it. He recognizes that when a culture's key beliefs are given up, *everything falls*, and he recognizes that the culture's key beliefs are inextricably linked to its mythology. The West, having killed not only its own central myth but all myth in general, has sealed its own fate. The question of how to intervene and prevent this collapse is the problem JP is trying to resolve, the puzzle that he has been working on.

We haven't yet arrived at a clear problem statement, however. For this, let's turn to the very opening of MoM. Here is how JP opens the first chapter:

The world can be validly construed as forum for action, or as place of things.

41

The former manner of interpretation—more primordial, and less clearly understood—finds its expression in the arts or humanities, in ritual, drama, literature, and mythology. The world as forum for action is a place of value, a place where all things have meaning. This meaning, which is shaped as a consequence of social interaction, is implication for action, or—at a higher level of analysis—implication for the configuration of the interpretive schema that produces or guides action.

The latter manner of interpretation—the world as place of things—finds its formal expression in the methods and theories of science. Science allows for increasingly precise determination of the consensually-validatable properties of things, and for efficient utilization of precisely-determined things as tools (once the direction such use is to take has been determined, through application of more fundamental narrative processes).

No complete world-picture can be generated, without use of both modes of construal. The fact that one mode is generally set at odds with the other means only that the nature of their respective domains remains insufficiently discriminated. Adherents of the mythological world-view tend to regard the statements of their creeds as indistinguishable from empirical "fact," even though such statements were generally formulated long before the notion of objective reality emerged. Those who, by contrast, accept the scientific perspective—who assume that it is, or might become, complete—forget that an impassable gulf currently divides what is from what should be.

What we find is that JP provides us with a clear problem statement within the opening paragraphs of MoM. What it boils down to is that there are two fundamental worldviews in the West, the scientific and the religious. The problem is that a *complete world-picture* requires both world-views but, currently at least, these two world-views have been *set at odds* with each other, treated as mutually incompatible. If you've ever wondered why JP quotes the Bible so much, it's because he is trying to resolve this problem. He recognizes that both worldviews must somehow be reconciled with each other in order to ensure the preservation of the West's key beliefs and ensure the furtherance of Western culture; or worded another way, to prevent the inevitable collapse of the culture.

On that note, we should probably get clear about what the collapse of Western culture actually means within this context. The collapse of a culture is an event that corresponds to the collapse of that culture's value hierarchy. So the collapse of Western culture would mean the abandonment of its key belief, of its central assumption. Once that assumption is no longer believed and acted on, the original culture has essentially died and been replaced by something else. Worded this way, most Westerners would be hard-pressed to find something worth worrying about. After all, we are only talking about the collapse of a belief system and that doesn't seem to be that big a deal. But this mindset only exists because people fail to recognize what the West stands to lose from the death or extinction of its key belief. JP, however, knows precisely what is at stake and what we would lose: *The idea of the divine individual took thousands of years to fully develop, and is still constantly threatened by direct attack and insidious counter-movement. It is based upon realization that the individual is the locus of experience.*

The nature of the solution

The idea of the divine individual underpins everything that the West holds dear, like individual human rights. This is what JP is trying to defend and protect. He's motivated to do so because he recognizes the value of the idea and the purpose that it serves in defining and maintaining the culture in which he finds himself, but he also sees that the idea is constantly being threatened. JP goes further, though, as he tells us what this idea is based on and it's this realization that is so vital. That realization is that *the individual is the locus of experience.* The significance of this last point can't be overstated. This realization both underpins the idea of the divine individual and also hints at the nature of the solution. And while this idea is very hard to explain, it's relatively easy to illustrate using the pattern of the *"hero's quest"*:

> *The hero's quest or journey has been represented in mythology and ritual in numerous ways, but the manifold representations appear in accordance with the myth of the way, as previously described: a harmonious community or way of life, predictable and stable in structure and function, is unexpectedly threatened by the emergence of (previously harnessed) unknown and dangerous forces. An individual of humble and princely origins rises, by free choice, to counter this threat. This individual is exposed to great personal trials, and risks or experiences physical and psychological dissolution. Nonetheless, he overcomes the threat, is magically restored (frequently improved) and receives a great reward, in consequence. He returns to his community with the reward, and (re)establishes social order (sometimes after a crisis engendered by his return).*

– Maps of Meaning

Imagine that a problem of a fairly serious and threatening nature exists but no one, that is, no individual took responsibility for solving the problem. Unless this problem magically resolves itself, something that is very unlikely, without anyone working at its resolution, the problem is guaranteed to persist and even get worse. "An unsolved problem seldom sits there, in stasis. It grows new heads, like a hydra" (Beyond Order). And so, the hero's quest begins with a problem that needs to be solved. What's easy to miss, however, is that an individual is required in order to solve the problem. The problem manifests itself as the emergence of a threat. The hero, an individual, recognizes the threat and rises to counter that threat. The hero, again an individual, takes responsibility for the problem.

When an individual takes responsibility for a problem, an as yet unsolved problem, he embarks on a journey that is challenging in proportion to the size of the problem that he has picked up. The act of picking up an unresolved problem with the intention of resolving that problem defines the journey. Picking up the problem moves the individual from the domain of the known to the domain of the unknown as an unresolved problem, by definition, is one for which a solution is not yet known. What's more—and this cannot be overstated—there is absolutely no guarantee that the individual will succeed at solving the problem. Simply picking up a problem does not guarantee success in resolving it. The individual must contend with the problem earnestly if he is ever going to solve it. And should he succeed in solving it, the process will invariably transform him as the conflict of ideas is resolved within him. JP expresses these ideas this way:

> The hero is the first person to have his "internal structure" (that is, his hierarchy of values and his behaviors) reorganized as a consequence of contact with an emergent anomaly. His "descent into the underworld" and subsequent reorganization makes him a savior—but his contact with the dragon of chaos also contaminates him with the forces that disrupt tradition and stability. The reigning "status-quo" stability may be only apparent—that is, the culture in its present form may already be doomed by as-of-yet not fully manifested change. The hero detects the dragon, or at least admits to its presence, before anyone else, and leads the charge.
>
> – Maps of Meaning

We catch a hint of the idea that the individual is the locus of experience reflected in the idea that the hero is the first to have his internal structure reorganized. What this means is that a problem is not resolved "out there" somewhere but within an individual. Only an individual can pick up a problem. Only an individual can contend with a problem, because contending with a problem is something that can only happen within the individual. This means that the conflicting ideas, or "opposites" that constitute the problem, must first be resolved within the individual, within a "single breast" as it were. Only an individual can... *attempt to live out the myth of the hero within the confines of individual personality—to voluntarily shoulder the cross of existence, to "unite the opposites" within a single breast, and to serve as active conscious mediator between the eternal generative forces of known and unknown.* The hero is that single breast that opens itself up to the problem, invites it in, contends with and, if successful, resolves the conflict. The individual, therefore, acts as host to this process within himself. That's what it means to *serve as active conscious mediator*. The problem requires a host of this kind for its resolution. There is simply no getting around the necessity of the individual in resolving a problem of this nature, even in our modern world, because the individual is the locus of experience.

Setting the scene

We need to examine one more element of JP's thinking in order to form a clear picture of how everything fits together. That element is the paradigmatic structure of the known and of culture. As a starting point consider the following statement from MoM:

> *The revolutionary hero is the individual who decides voluntarily, courageously, to face some aspect of the still-unknown and threatening. He may also be the only person who is presently capable of perceiving that social adaptation is incompletely or improperly structured, in a particular way—who presently understands that there still remain unconquered evil spirits, dangerous unknowns and threatening possibilities. In taking creative action, he (re) encounters chaos, generates new myth-predicated behavioral strategies, and extends the boundaries (or transforms the paradigmatic structure) of cultural competence.*

Notice that the revolutionary hero brings about a particular type of change. That change is described as a transformation of the paradigmatic structure of cultural competence. Earlier we saw that the hero is the first person to have his internal structure reorganized. In both of these cases, the structure that is being referred to is paradigmatic. A basic grasp of what JP means by paradigmatic structure is therefore critical to this discussion, and so let's turn to MoM once again:

> *A paradigm is a complex cognitive tool, whose use presupposes acceptance of a limited number of axioms (or definitions of what constitutes reality, for the purposes of argument and action), whose interactions produce an internally consistent explanatory and predictive structure... Human culture has, by necessity, a para-digmatic structure—devoted not towards objective description of what is, but to description of the cumulative affective relevance, or meaning, of what is.*

Without unpacking any of this, we're going to take note of a few things. We want to note that culture has a paradigmatic structure. In light of this, we can see that the two valid ways that the world can be construed are also, therefore, by necessity, paradigmatic structure, as JP articulates this way:

> *Explicitly scientific paradigmatic systems... are concerned with the prediction and control of events whose existence can be ver-ified, in a particular formal manner, and offer "model problems and solutions to a community of practitioners." Pre-experimental thinking—which primarily means moral thinking [thinking about the meaning or significance of events (objects and behaviors)]— also appears necessarily characterized by paradigmatic structure.*

Why is this important and what does this have to do with the hero? Well, looking back at the problem statement, we see that the two ways in which the world can be validly construed constitute paradigmatic structures. These structures are based on a different set of axioms that make them incom-patible with each other. Despite this inconvenient fact, both worldviews, both paradigmatic structures, are necessary for a complete world-picture. When the problem is framed this way, we get a hint at what it will take to move forward: *Movement from one schema to another—or from both to a hypothetical third, which unites both (which might constitute the consequence*

*of revolutionary heroic effort)—presupposes dissolution (mutual or singular)—
not mere addition (presupposes a "qualitative" shift, not a "quantitative" shift).*

The West is currently of two minds, split into two different schemas or paradigmatic structures that correspond to the two valid ways to construe the world: scientific and moral thinking. What this implies is that we have the option to pick one of the existing worldviews and "move" to it or we must find a third that unites both of the existing schemas. The paradigmatic structure of these worldviews ensures that these three options are the only valid options available to us. There is no middle ground. But, as we've already seen, neither existing paradigm is complete without the other. We can't form a complete world picture without both of these. What this means is that picking one of the existing paradigms and moving to it doesn't constitute a solution. This is worth repeating, because most people who identify with the scientific worldview fail to appreciate that their worldview is incomplete without the religious worldview. And, sadly enough, the same can be said of many, if not most, in the other direction. Regardless, however, the salient point is that transforming a religious culture into a secular culture comes at a cost and we've already noted that, in the case of the West, the cost would be the loss of its key belief in the divinity of the individual. And we've seen what that would do for us. Clearly, movement in the other direction isn't a workable idea either. The process of elimination leads us naturally to a very troubling conclusion, which is that there is only one valid way forward. Somehow, if Western culture is to avoid seeing its key belief become extinct, it must somehow find a schema that unites both of the current schemas. But this implies a dissolution of both existing views.

This brings us back to the hero, the first person to have his internal structure reorganized. Owing to the fact that the individual is the locus of experience, we know that this movement forward must first take place within an individual. The way this works is detailed in MoM. Without getting into the specifics, what JP tells us is that the individual first internalizes the paradigmatic structure of his culture. JP calls this process enculturation and adds that it is achieved through apprenticeship. Only once the individual has internalized his culture's structure is he ready to face the emergent threat, resolve the struggle of opposites within himself, and then bring the processed information back, making it possible for others to follow in his footsteps. That is how movement forward happens, must happen because of the paradigmatic structure of culture. For culture to move forward, this structural change must first take place within one of its members, an individual. All of this is present in the idea that the hero is the first to have his internal structure reorganized. Once the hero's internal structure has successfully been reorganized, and the nature of this reorganized structure is successfully communicated to his culture, the way forward becomes visible, and more importantly, accessible.

Tying all of these ideas together we see that the emergent threat within the West is the scientific worldview. We may not think of this threat as emergent, because it's been around for a few hundred years already. Nevertheless, this threat has killed or, more accurately, is continuing to kill our culture's central myth. That is, the change brought about by the emergence of the *world as place of things* worldview has been playing out for centuries and is still doing so. *The reigning "status-quo" stability may be only apparent—that is, the culture in its present form may already be doomed by as-of-yet not fully manifested change.*

It should be obvious, at this point, that the death of a culture's central myth will eventually lead to the collapse of that culture. What this means, for the West, is that *the culture in its present form* not only *may already be*, but actually is *doomed by as-of-yet not fully manifested change.* If this change is permitted to run its course, the idea of the divinity of the individual will be lost and Western culture dissolved. That's why what the West needs in the current moment is a revolutionary hero, someone who *opens himself up to the possibility of advancement—to furtherance of his culture's central myth:*

> *The individual troubled by anomalous and anxiety-provoking experiential data is suffering equally from the "disintegration," "rigidity" or "senility" of the society within. The choice to "process"*

such data—that is, to "mine" it for significance, and to destabilize the socially-constructed intrapsychic hierarchy of behavior and values, in consequence—is equivalent, mythologically speaking, to the "descent to the underworld." If this descent is successful— that is, if the exploring individual does not retreat to his previous personality structure, and wall himself in, and if he does not fall prey to hopelessness, anxiety and despair—then he may "return" to the community, treasure in hand, with processed information whose incorporation would benefit the remaining members of society. It is very likely, however, that he will be viewed with fear and even hatred, as a consequence of his "contamination with the unknown"—particularly if those "left behind" are "unconscious" of the threat that motivated his original journey.

– Maps of Meaning

Processed information

In a sense, we've been laying the groundwork, not only for the remainder of this chapter but for the remainder of the book. We'll be coming back to a number of these ideas in the following chapters. At this point, however, we should have a good enough sense of the problem statement and the limiting constraints that the paradigmatic structure of the known imposes on the solution. That should be all we need to jump directly to the particular goal of this chapter. To do that, let's turn our attention to the treasure that the successful revolutionary hero returns with. This treasure, JP tells us, comes in the form of *processed information*.

Earlier I claimed to be in possession of the missing piece of the puzzle that JP has been working on. This piece of the puzzle constitutes my *treasure in hand,* which is a direct result of a *successful descent.* Together, the fact that my life conforms to the pattern of the hero myth coupled with this treasure, serve as evidence that I've been cast to play the role of cultural revolutionary hero. In theory, this missing piece of the puzzle should really be sufficient evidence in itself. The fact that I came to possess the missing piece in the way that I did, coupled with the fact that I figured out how it fits into the puzzle, serve as corroborating evidence.

As for the descent itself, I've already stated that it began in 2004, when at the age of 40 I made the conscious decision to walk away from God. Of course, back then, I didn't know anything about this idea of a call to adventure. I didn't know anything about the nihilistic void and the abyss. I didn't know anything about the hero's quest and the pattern that it followed. I didn't know any of that. The only thing I knew for sure was that I was choosing to walk away from God and that that constituted making a conscious decision to spend eternity in hell. That was the extent to which I could say that I *peered into the abyss* before jumping in.

> *When you peer into an abyss, you see a monster. If it is a small abyss, then it is a small monster. But if it is the ultimate abyss, then it is the ultimate monster. That is certainly a dragon—perhaps even the dragon of evil itself.*
>
> – Beyond Order

By my estimation, the descent took five years. At that point, I found myself swallowed whole by the beast that resides at the bottom of that ultimate abyss. I'd chosen to spend eternity in hell, expecting that that eternity would start only at my death. This was a massive error on my part and I found myself living in hell far sooner than expected. My time in hell started as soon as I'd been consumed by the dragon. What that meant is that all notions of meaning and purpose evaporated in the absence of God. I became nihilistic through and through, and with that life ceased being worth living. What JP says about Nietzsche in *Beyond Order* could just as easily have been said about me at this time: *Nietzsche appears to have unquestioningly adopted the idea that the world was both objective and valueless in the manner posited by the emergent physical sciences.* By 2012, I'd been trapped within this monster for something like three years. The experience was like living in a sort of quicksand of anger, bitterness, and resentment. Without purpose or meaning, everything was a struggle that served only to pull me further and further down. I was trapped and I knew it and, having thoroughly burned my bridges, there was no going back. There was no going back and there was no way forward, at least none that I could see.

After three very long years in this state, in March of 2012, I came into contact with something that corresponds to JP's idea of discovering my *dead father* there in the belly of the beast. The encounter itself took place at a large, work-related conference that I was attending in Houston, Texas. I was there to acquire technical information relating to a significant project I was working on. Despite this, as I browsed through the various lectures that were on offer, I found myself drawn to a lecture that fell completely outside of the technology stream. The lecture was titled "Responsibility Redefined" and the speaker's name was Christopher Avery.[6]

The title and description of this lecture called to me. And so, at the appointed time, I found myself in a lecture hall with a few hundred others, waiting to hear what Christopher had to say. Christopher began to speak and I watched and listened as he brought Responsibility into the spotlight, clarifying what it most certainly was not and illuminating what it was. He spoke of Responsibility not in terms of taking responsibility for this or for that but as a mindset, what JP might call a mode of being or perhaps even a *pattern of action, imagination and thought.* But here's where it gets really interesting. Christopher Avery (CA) talked of Responsibility not as something you did but as a process at work within each of us. That's right—a process! This idea of Responsibility as process was entirely new to me.

While the title of the lecture was Responsibility Redefined, what Christopher Avery presented wasn't so much a definition of Responsibility as a model of Responsibility. He even had a name for this model. He called it, appropriately enough, "The Responsibility Process" and spoke of it as leading to the adoption of 100% Responsibility in your life.

---

6   While details like this may seem merely coincidental, I can't help but marvel at the fact that this man's name, Christopher, comes from the Greek Christophoros, which literally means "Christ-bearing."

A pause is in order here to appreciate just how on the nose this is. If you're familiar with JP, you know just how central a role responsibility plays in his thinking. Here's just a sample, from Beyond Order:

> What is the antidote to the suffering and malevolence of life? The highest possible goal. What is the prerequisite to pursuit of the highest possible goal? Willingness to adopt the maximum degree of responsibility—and this includes the responsibilities that others disregard or neglect.

The Responsibility Process, the model itself was extremely simple yet profoundly so. To say that it resonated with me wouldn't begin to describe how I felt as I listened to Christopher speak about and then, with audience participation, demonstrate just how effective the model was at leading people to adopt this mode of being, this mindset he called Responsibility. At the time, I was miserable and I knew it but Christopher's conception of Responsibility, The Responsibility Process, was like a spotlight cutting through the dense fog of confusion that I'd gotten swallowed up by.

Christopher's presentation was, for anyone paying attention, more than just a lecture. It was a call to Responsibility. For me, however, it was much, much more than that. This call to Responsibility was an echo of the call to follow Christ that I'd answered in my early twenties. I responded in the same way to this latter call as I had the former, not merely intellectually but with the intention of living it, or in JP's words, of embodying it, fully. That is, something in me was responding to what I was hearing and that response felt nearly exactly the same as my response to the Gospel. I recognized the effect almost immediately, though at the time I didn't know how to make sense of it and, in fact, wouldn't manage to make complete sense of it till I discovered JP's conception of Christ more than six years into the ascent back to the surface. But the ascent itself began with that lecture.

The Responsibility Process

...the meaning that sustains people through difficult times is to be found not so much in happiness, which is fleeting, but in in the voluntary adoption of mature responsibility for the self and others.

– Beyond Order

The Responsibility Process, CA informs us, is a process that is at work within us. In CA's own words, The Responsibility Process is *a little-known pattern in our minds that determines how we process thoughts about taking and avoiding responsibility.* We saw, in the previous chapter, that JP's conception of Christ represented a *pattern of action, imagination and thought;* and here we have CA telling us that The Responsibility Process is a *pattern in our minds.* What's more, since this pattern deals specifically with thoughts about *taking and avoiding responsibility,* this pattern in our minds produces a pattern of action, or behavior once we've chosen to either take or avoid responsibility. And so, in CA's description of The Responsibility Process we see a very strong correlation with JP's *pattern of action, imagination and thought, or Christ.*

It's critically important to realize that this process isn't always active. Much of the time it's dormant, waiting to be activated, to *kick in* when needed. The obvious implication is that this process is not always visible. So we must first learn to recognize the conditions under which it is. CA provides us with the answer: *When we have what we want, we are winning. When we feel blocked and stopped from having what we want, then we get anxious, frustrated, and upset—and then The Responsibility Process kicks in...* And, just in case you're wondering just how big an upset you need to experience before this process is activated, he adds, *Remember, the trigger that kicks off The Responsibility Process is an upset of any size.* We see then, that The Responsibility Process is activated by an upset, an upset of any size. So, if we want to observe this process at work within us we must watch for the trigger, the upset, because that's when this *little known pattern in our own minds* kicks in and becomes visible to us.

What we've just learned about how CA's The Responsibility Process (TRP) is activated by an *upset* is tremendously significant because CA's upset maps directly to something in MoM. Anyone who's read MoM should easily recognize the connection between CA's upset and JP's anomaly. While the words being used are different, the two ideas themselves are equivalent or interchangeable. This connection between CA's upset and JP's anomaly is so important that it's worth taking a closer look.

Consider how CA tells us that, *When we have what we want, we are winning.* JP tells us that *it is the production of what we want that we use as evidence for the integrity of our knowledge.* JP tells us, point blank, that we *compare what is happening to what we want—to what we desire to be.* So we see that both men are saying the same thing. CA provides only minimal information about these upsets because we all know an upset when we experience one, but JP puts this upset under a microscope so to speak. Here's how he describes our response to an anomaly, to something unexpected, something we don't want:

> *If something unknown or unpredictable occurs, while we are carrying out our motivated plans, we are first surprised. That surprise— which is a combination of apprehension and curiosity—comprises our instinctive emotional response to the occurrence of something we did not desire. The appearance of something unexpected is proof that we do not know how to act—by definition, as it is the production of what we want that we use as evidence for the integrity of our knowledge. If we are somewhere we don't know how to act, we are (probably) in trouble—we might learn something new, but we are still in trouble. When we are in trouble, we get scared. When we are in the domain of the known, so to speak, there is no reason for fear. Outside that domain, panic reigns. It is for this reason that we dislike having our plans disrupted.*

> – Maps of Meaning

We see CA's ideas mirrored perfectly in JP's ideas right down to the fine details. For example, JP expresses CA's idea that *an upset of any size* can trigger TRP this way: *The appearance of anomaly can be less or more upsetting.* Here we see a convergence, not only of ideas but of terminology. Most critically, perhaps, both of these ideas point to biological responses. It's clear that CA is directing our attention to a biological process at work within us that manifests itself at the emergence of an upset. This corresponds to JP's *pattern of instinctive response* in the following: *Human beings are prepared, biologically, to respond to anomalous information—to novelty... This pattern of instinctive response drives learning—particularly, but not exclusively, the learning of appropriate behavior. All such learning takes place—or took place originally—as a consequence of contact with novelty, or anomaly.* JP tells us we are biologically prepared to respond to anomaly and CA tells us that TRP is a vital part of that response mechanism.

TRP is about how we respond to upsets and now that we understand how the idea relates to JP's anomaly, we can more clearly see the reflection of JP's conception of Christ in TRP. What's more, we've taken careful note that this *little-known process* is specifically concerned with taking or abdicating responsibility. The connection between CA's upset and JP's anomaly enables us to see JP's hero and adversary mirrored in CA's idea of taking or abdicating of Responsibility, as they both represent two different attitudes toward the unknown. Every upset, therefore, is an opportunity, an opportunity to choose which of these two we want to embody.

Anomaly is, therefore, spiritual "food" in the most literal sense: the unknown is the raw material out of which the personality is manufactured, in the course of exploratory activity. The act of rejecting anomaly transforms the personality into something starved, something senile, and something increasingly terrified of change, as each failure to face the truth undermines capacity to face truth in the future. The man who comes to adopt an inappropriate attitude towards the unknown severs his connection with the source of all knowledge, undermining his personality, perhaps irreparably.

– Maps of Meaning

We like to say "every upset is an opportunity to learn."

– The Responsibility Process

In the set or outside?

It is primordial separation of light from darkness—engendered by Logos, the Word, equivalent to the process of consciousness—that initiates human experience and historical activity, which is reality itself, for all intents and purposes. This initial division provides the prototypic structure, and the fundamental precondition, for the elaboration and description of more differentiated attracting and repulsing pairs of opposites...

– Maps of Meaning

Now that we've established a firm connection between CA's TRP process and JP's ideas, let's consider the ways in which TRP corresponds to the process that produces the Mandelbrot set. Recall that the process that generates the Mandelbrot set consists of iterating a point through a simple function and asking ourselves if the total is running off to infinity or remaining finite. What we see is that this process categorizes the behavior of each point into one of two fundamental categories, stable or unstable. The behavior of each point determines if the point belongs in or outside of the set. This conscious aspect of the process serves to discriminate, to differentiate. It observes the behavior and then rejects points that demonstrate one type of behavior while accepting points that demonstrate a different type of behavior. It's here, in this simple act of discriminating between these two fundamental categories of behavior, that the similarities between the process that generates the Mandelbrot set and TRP can most clearly be seen.

TRP also uses two fundamental categories and requires that we discriminate between the two. Only what we are discriminating between in TRP process, constitute mindsets. In TRP, Responsibility is a mindset and the abdication of Responsibility is a mindset. Behavior plays a part, but since it's the *pattern of thought in our minds* that drives behavior, we will focus on that. TRP tells us that there are two fundamental patterns that these thoughts in our minds conform to. These two fundamental patterns correspond to either taking or abdicating responsibility. Armed with the understanding that CA's idea of an upset corresponds to JP's idea of an anomaly, which itself constitutes the unknown, we see JP's two *archetypes of response to the unknown* built into TRP. What we see, then, is that CA's two fundamental mindsets map to JP's two eternal tendencies: *The mythic "hostile brothers"—Spenta Mainyu and Angra Mainyu, Osiris and Seth, Gilgamesh and Enkidu, Cain and Abel, Christ and Satan—are representative of two eternal individual tendencies, twin "sons of god," heroic and adversarial.* And having already tied JP's mythological *hostile brothers* to their counterparts, stable and unstable orbits, in the process that generates the Mandelbrot set, we've successfully demonstrated how all three of these processes are equivalent at a very fundamental level.

Let's consider these two patterns of thought, these two tendencies. In MoM, these two tendencies are archetypal patterns that manifest or play out within each individual. That's why JP describes them as *eternal individual tendencies*, because they play out or manifest themselves at the level or scale of the individual.

> *The heroic tendency—the archetypal savior—is an eternal spirit, which is to say, a central and permanent aspect of human being. The same is true, precisely, of the "adversarial" tendency: the capacity for endless denial, and the desire to make everything suffer for the outrage of its existence, is an ineradicable intrapsychic element of the individual.*

JP's two tendencies are themselves categories, categories of archetypal "way[s] of being in the face of the unknown." And these two tendencies map directly to CA's two fundamental mindsets: Responsibility and abdication of Responsibility, which CA calls Coping. Both of these, we'll recall, are mindsets. Coping, therefore, maps to the adversarial tendency that either denies or runs away from the unknown. *Rejection of the unknown is tantamount to "identification with the devil," the mythological counterpart and eternal adversary of the world-creating exploratory hero."* Responsibility, obviously, maps to the heroic tendency. *The exploratory hero, divine son of the known and unknown, courageously faces the unknown...*

Across the board, we have three descriptions of processes that discriminate and sort between two fundamental categories. Stable orbits map to the heroic tendency, which maps to Responsibility; while unstable orbits map to the adversarial tendency, which maps to Coping. The terms differ but they represent the same things, the same two categories or patterns. Nevertheless, the term that CA uses to represent the adversarial tendency calls for further exploration since we don't tend to think or talk about Coping as something that is as negative as the adversarial tendency. That is, we don't instinctively see Responsibility and Coping as two *warring opposites.*

Coping, in this culture, is often portrayed as a good thing. If we hear, for instance, that someone is coping well with something, we interpret this as good news. But, if Coping constitutes the opposite of Responsibility, then we must be confused about Coping's true nature. Let's see if we can burn off some of the confusion by sharpening the contrast between Responsibility and Coping. What we want to know, basically, is how to discriminate between these two mindsets. Once we clearly see these constitute warring opposites, we'll be properly motivated to discriminate between them.

Let's start by examining both JP's and CA's thinking about Coping, starting with JP in *Beyond Order: This might be regarded as a philosophy of responsibility. A responsible person decides to make a problem his or her problem, and then works diligently—even ambitiously—for its solution..."* We can see that JP is telling us that the defining characteristic of responsibility is the adoption of problems with the intention of resolving them. Thinking in terms of opposites, it isn't hard to see that the opposite of Responsibility can be as simple and seemingly benign as doing nothing, simply not taking ownership of the problem, simply leaving the problem unsolved. And we might think to ourselves, well what's so bad about that? Fortunately, JP answers this question: *An unsolved problem seldom sits there, in stasis. It grows new heads, like a hydra... Thus, your refusal or even inability to come to terms with the errors of the past expands the source of such error—expands the unknown that surrounds you, transforms that unknown into something increasingly predatory.* But that's not all. JP continues:

> *And, while that is happening, you get weaker. You are less than you could be because you did not change. You did not become who you could have become as a consequence of that change— and worse: you have now taught yourself, by your own example, that such turning away is acceptable, and you are therefore more likely to commit the same error in the future. And what you failed to face is now larger. This is not the kind of causal process, the kind of positive feedback loop, that you want to find yourself trapped within.*

– Maps of Meaning

Perhaps Coping isn't as benign as it appears. But, until we see Coping for what it is, the opposite of Responsibility, we risk thinking of Coping as an acceptable *mode of being*. Doing so means failing to recognize that Coping represents the very opposite of the heroic tendency. This lack of discrimination leaves us open to adopting and embodying the adversarial tendency without realizing it and, more importantly, without feeling bad about it. This brings to light something that JP fails to stress about the adversarial spirit, and that it is just how extremely subtle it can be (Genesis 3:1). Awareness of the subtle nature of the adversarial tendency is necessary, therefore, in order to avoid mindlessly embodying the wrong tendency. We need to be absolutely clear about the fact that Coping is, very literally, the abdication of, the denial of personal responsibility. And then we must allow JP's words to resonate in our minds: "The most dangerous lie of all is devoted towards denial of individual responsibility..."

Now that we're clear about JP's thinking with respect to Coping, let's turn our attention to CA. We'll start with CA's definition of responsibility:

What is Responsibility? Responsibility is a mental state that is open, spacious, free, and safe. You trust that you have sufficient intelligence, creativity, and resources to face whatever life brings. Where the other states are restrictive, this one is spacious, giving you room to think and explore. In the other states, you feel constrained or trapped, but in Responsibility you are free to choose and free from preconceived ideas about the problem or solution. You are free to reexamine what you want, free to just be.

– *The Responsibility Process*

The first thing that should jump out at us is that Responsibility is a mental state, a mindset, and not any particular action or behavior. We've seen this already, of course, but it's worth reiterating, because CA's conception of Responsibility is not what we typically think of when we see or hear the word. For that reason, CA capitalizes the word (as we've been doing) in order to emphasize the distinction. The next thing we need to address is CA's use of the phrase *other states*. We've spent some time stressing the fact that TRP discriminates between two and only two fundamental categories of mindsets, Responsibility and Coping, and here CA seems to be referring to other mental states. We'll see, shortly, that TRP includes six subcategories of Coping and this explains his use of the phrase. But that CA recognizes two, and only two, fundamental categories of mindsets is made clear when, speaking of Responsibility, he states: *Operating from any other mental state means coping with the problem rather than owning and solving it. Only in Responsibility can you release yourself from that frustration or upset.* So we see that there is Responsibility and there is *any other state,* and we see that operating from these other states *means Coping.*

Before moving on, we should take a quick look at the qualitative difference between these two fundamental mindsets. You get a pretty good sense of just how different Coping is from Responsibility from CA's description of how we feel when we inhabit them. When we are operating from Responsibility, we feel free and we act from a set of assumptions that make exploratory behavior possible. More precisely, when operating from Responsibility, we face the unknown courageously. On the other hand, when we operate from any other mental state, that is when we operate from Coping—we feel trapped, without choice, and not at all sufficient to face the unknown. It should be obvious, then, that even when we are Coping as best we can, we are still Coping with the problem rather than solving it. And, as CA points out, *we don't realize how much coping we are doing instead of problem solving—until we become attuned to it.*

Becoming attuned implies learning to discriminate between the two. Once we become attuned to it and we become clear about the fact that Coping constitutes abdication of Responsibility, then every upset becomes an opportunity because, as JP points out in *Beyond Order,* "Opportunity lurks where Responsibility has been abdicated."[7] TRP draws a clear line between Responsibility and Coping, and by doing so it *shows us how we get stuck in mental states where we cope with problems rather than solve them for good. And it shows us that the mental state of Responsibility is available to us— always, even when we think it isn't.*

Mindsets = Paradigms

Having firmly established the fact that TRP discriminates between two and only two fundamental categories, Responsibility and Coping, we are ready to take a closer look at TRP. Earlier we mentioned that TRP breaks Coping down into six subcategories. At this point it's worth applying what we've

---

7   Rule IV.

seen about the paradigmatic structure of the known to these six Coping mindsets in order to see that each constitutes a distinct paradigm. Recall that a *paradigm is a complex cognitive tool, whose use presupposes acceptance of a limited number of axioms... whose interactions produce an internally consistent explanatory and predictive structure.* Compare that to how CA describes these mindsets. Each mindset *is a mental state characterized by its point of view,* and *in each mental state, the cause-and-effect logic we apply is different.* We see in in these words all of the elements of JP's *internally consistent explanatory and predictive structure.* Furthermore, JP tells us that *Paradigmatic thinking might be described as thinking whose domain has been formally limited; thinking that acts "as if" some questions have been answered in a final manner."* This is consistent with CA's description of how we feel when operating from a Coping mindset: "Our reasoning is simplistic and restricted by the mental state" and "Our logic is mechanical, looking at simplistic cause and effect."

Recognizing that these mindsets have a paradigmatic structure allows us to borrow some of JP's ideas to better understand what we're dealing with here. For instance, JP tells us that:

> *Paradigmatic thinking allows for comprehension of an infinity of "facts," through application of a finite system of presuppositions— allows, in the final analysis, for the limited subject to formulate sufficient provisional understanding of the unlimited experiential object (including the subject).*

Our minds are continually making sense of the world, or at least the world we are facing at any given moment. To deal with the infinitely complex reality that we face, our minds make sense of things by first assuming some things to be true and then building a view of sorts, complete with *cause-and-effect logic* from these assumptions. What this means is that each mindset is simply a view, a limited view, constructed from a small set of unquestioned axioms along with some basic rules about how to think within this view. Recognizing the paradigmatic structure of these mindsets allows us to think of them correctly, to recognize them for what they are, a game: "In some regards, a paradigm is like a game. Play is optional, but, once undertaken, must be governed by (socially-verified) rules. These rules cannot be questioned, while the game is on..."

TRP in action

When we have what we want, we are winning. When we feel blocked and stopped from having what we want, then we get anxious, frustrated, and upset—and then The Responsibility Process kicks in and the coping patterns start.

– The Responsibility Process

As we've seen, TRP is triggered by an upset or the appearance of anomaly, to use JP's terminology. This is to say that TRP kicks in when the mind encounters something unwanted or unexpected, which is to say, something that doesn't make sense. This experience of things not making sense generates anxiety, and the mind responds by attempting to make sense of things, and that as quickly as possible. And it does just that. It makes sense of things and then transmits that meaning to your consciousness in the form of a paradigm, which is to say, a limited but internally consistent view, built on a small set of unquestioned assumptions. This view, as we've seen, comes complete with its own *cause-and-effect logic* for the problem. That is to say, the mind offers up a game, a game complete with a set of rules that are, from within the game, logically consistent.

Our minds respond to the appearance of anomaly by trying to make sense of things. This, it must be stressed, happens automatically. If we're not aware of this, it's all too easy to conflate this paradigm offered up from our subconscious with the truth. This mistake is understandable since the paradigm appears as a whole, complete with its own set of axioms and internal logic and therefore the paradigm provides a sense of meaning even if based on false assumptions. This fact renders each paradigm persuasive enough to trick us into accepting the game and start playing it. The problem, however, is that what makes sense can just as easily be grounded on lies (false axioms), as is always the case with Coping mindsets.

If we're unaware of this, it's all too easy to confuse the product of this unconscious sense-making process, the paradigm that it sends up to our conscious mind, with the truth. It's the job of the conscious mind, however, to check the solution as it were, before accepting the paradigm as good enough. Failure to recognize that the unconscious mind may not be serving up the most accurate, the most truthful view of reality, will result in simply accepting the paradigm and acting on it as though it were the truth. When this happens, we find ourselves playing a game in which we accept the axioms and rules unquestioningly. Furthermore, if the paradigm constitutes a Coping mindset, then we find ourselves playing a degenerating game, all while thinking we are operating from the truth.

Comparing this to the process that generates the Mandelbrot set, we can think of the unconscious mind as running the calculation and sending the answer up to the conscious mind. It's the conscious mind's responsibility, or job, to examine the result and to discriminate, or categorize that result. In the case of the Mandelbrot set, this corresponds to discriminating between stable and unstable behavior. In the case of TRP, this corresponds to discriminating between Coping and Responsibility mindsets. Furthermore, it's the conscious mind's job, not only to discriminate but to actively reject Coping mindsets in the same way that points that demonstrate unstable orbits are plotted as not in the set. This final step in the process is critical. Failure to discriminate can have catastrophic consequences; as CA points out, "You can get stuck in any mental state around a problem for a moment, minute, day, month, year, decade, or lifetime." Just imagine a lifetime spent coping with problems but never resolving them, and you get a glimpse of a rather pitiful existence. This is certainly *not the kind of causal process, the kind of positive feedback loop, which you want to find yourself trapped within.* In this way, thinking of these mindsets as paradigms, as games, can help us remember that *play is optional.* We don't have to enter into the game and this is especially important to be aware of when the game itself is a degenerating game. We are always free to refuse to play.

This idea of entering into the game, of accepting its axioms as true, of acting out its rules, is all part of embodying the mindset. And since there are only two fundamental mindsets, what this means is that each upset results in a choice, a choice to either embody the heroic tendency or the adversarial tendency. Being aware of this enables us to determine, ahead of the upset, which pattern we most want to embody, and then, when the upset presents itself, this awareness creates the opportunity to consciously choose which we will actually embody. We can only do this, of course, if we can correctly discriminate between the two. This is precisely where TRP comes to our aid.

TRP draws a clear line between Coping and Responsibility. And by bringing Coping and Responsibility into sharp contrast, it teaches us to discriminate correctly. It provides us with a window into our own minds, not to mention hearts, in order to recognize our own attitude toward *taking and avoiding responsibility*. Becoming aware of this *little-known process in our minds* enables us to become aware of the *patterns of action, imagination, and thought* that we are embodying. "The lesson then is to pay attention to our own thoughts, language, and behaviors when we are upset or frustrated."

The Coping mindsets

Now that we are 100% clear on the fact that TRP is about discriminating between and embodying either Coping or Responsibility, we're ready to take a closer look at the subcategories of Coping. These subcategories represent specific patterns, whereas Coping represents the more general category that they belong to. Each of the following represents a particular expression or manifestation of Coping:

Denial

Lay Blame

Justify

Shame

Obligation

Quit

Looking at this list, it's easy to see why each of these is a subcategory of Coping. It isn't hard to see how each is incompatible with Responsibility. That is, these mindsets represent what Responsibility most surely is not. And so, operating from one of these mindsets constitutes Coping, constitutes the abdication of Responsibility. It's perhaps best to think of what we're doing here as drawing a clear line of discrimination between Coping and Responsibility by making what is not Responsibility clear. This idea of drawing a clear line of discrimination between our two categories of mindsets has its counterpart in the process that generates the Mandelbrot set. In the previous chapter, we talked about the distinction between those points that head off to infinity and those that remain finite, but we didn't mention that there is a clear "line" that is used to discriminate between these two behaviors.

This line or boundary is used by the programs that execute this process in order to display the Mandelbrot set. With reference to such a program, Gleick describes how to use this boundary line in order to discriminate between behaviors this way: *If the running total becomes greater than 2 or smaller than −2 in either its real or imaginary part, it is surely heading off to infinity—the program can move on.* It may not be obvious from this description but the line that Gleick is describing is the circumference of a circle of radius 2 about the origin. The line that constitutes the circumference of that circle acts as the cut-off line, or line of discrimination between stable and unstable orbits. The moment the calculation yields a result that falls outside this circle, it has "crossed the line." It must be rejected, plotted as not in the set. It doesn't require much thought to realize that the absence of such a line would mean that there would be no clear boundary beyond which we could know, with certainty, that the point is guaranteed to be heading off to infinity. In the absence of such a line of discrimination, differentiating between behaviors would be impossible. In a very similar fashion, without a clear boundary line that separates Responsibility from Coping, we would not be able to discriminate between the two and confusion would reign.

We've already seen that CA draws a clear line separating Responsibility from Coping. What we didn't mention is that this line is schematically represented on a chart developed by CA to represent TRP. On this chart, a literal line delineates between Responsibility, which he places at the top of the chart, and the six Coping mindsets which fall below the line. Here is how CA talks about this cut-off line.

> In the mental states below the line (Denial, Lay Blame, Justify, Shame, Obligation, Quit), we cope with problems and we talk, talk, talk about them, or obsess internally and even lose sleep, but we never solve them from these mental positions. Above the line (Responsibility) we grow to overcome problems.

If you're familiar with some of Einstein's most popular sayings, you might recognize, in these words, Einstein's idea that *No problem can be solved from the same level of consciousness that created it.* These ideas hint at something that CA doesn't cast enough light on. We catch a hint of it in Einstein's words. The point is that Coping constitutes the level of consciousness responsible for creating problems. This means that, not only do we not solve problems when operating from one of these Coping mindsets, but we actually create new problems when we act or speak from within any of these. This, of course, guarantees that the problems we create when operating from Coping will compound because we can't solve them from this level of consciousness. To solve the problems we invariably need to change levels of consciousness, we need to operate from a higher level of consciousness—which, of course, is Responsibility.

Drawing the line

Where precisely does the line that differentiates Coping from Responsibility lie? TRP places it within us. This means that the clearer we are about what constitutes crossing that line, the more clearly we will see where the boundary lies. Clarity, for its part, comes from learning to identify these Coping mindsets when they present themselves to us, calling us to buy-in, to accept their axioms, and start playing the limited game they represent. Play is optional, but unless we're conscious enough, we'll simply get swallowed up by one of these mindsets and never even notice. Once inside the mindset, it's easy to get stuck in the circular logic that's built into the game. And so, if we don't settle the matter ahead of time, before the upset manifests itself, we either won't know or won't care to discriminate and reject the mindset. We'll simply embody it. That is, unless we know that another game, a better game, exists and is always available, we're most likely to simply accept what appears, at the moment, to be the only option available.

The quickest way not only to learn to identify these Coping mindsets but to also develop a distaste for them is to listen to the stories we're telling ourselves. Recall from Chapter 1 that *We use stories to regulate our emotions and govern our behavior; use stories to provide the present we inhabit with a determinate point of reference—the desired future.* Well, these mindsets constitute *a determinate point of reference* or a view, as we've been calling it. Each mindset comes complete with its own narrative theme, and the stories we tell ourselves within each mindset can be recognized by this theme. In fact, the very labels that CA uses to identify each mindset can be considered the defining theme of the stories we tell ourselves from within the mindset. So, by paying particular attention to the theme of the stories in our minds when we become upset, we can more clearly see which mindset is currently playing itself out, which pattern is being enacted.

There's more to this idea, however. JP tells us that we use stories to orient ourselves to the desired future and, ideally, to the optimal desired future. The thing about these Coping mindsets, however, is that the stories we tell ourselves when operating from within these mindsets, not only do not point us towards the optimal desired future, but they actively point us in the wrong direction, away from that future and towards one that is, well, hellish in nature. Except perhaps for those who have a preference for the adversarial tendency, none of us enjoys listening to these stories as they loop endlessly in our minds. When these stories are spinning around in our minds, we feel stuck in a vicious circle, unable to free ourselves from the endless repeating theme. This endless repetition is analogous to running the process that produces the Mandelbrot set without ever checking to see if the running total goes off to infinity. In programming terms, this would amount to an endless loop. The function continues to iterate, over and over, with no conscious act of discrimination making the judgment call needed to bring the iterations to an end.

What we see then, is that TRP teaches us that Responsibility, which is equivalent to embodying the heroic principle, requires actively observing the pattern of thought that manifests in our minds when upset. Noticing how we feel when we believe the stories that are repeating, over and over again, as if by their own will, also helps in the process of discriminating Responsibility from Coping. Through the act of observing, of noticing, and finally, of classifying or categorizing our internal state, we find ourselves stepping outside of the mindset even if just for a moment. But that moment is more than opportunity enough for us to come to our senses and realize that we wouldn't choose this mindset consciously. The moment we become aware of this we have an opportunity to reject the mindset, an opportunity to settle the matter within ourselves not to embody it, not to say or do anything from within this mindset, no matter how tempting. This is far from a trivial matter, because speaking and acting from within the mindset only reinforces it, making it progressively harder to escape its grip. This is because when we speak or act from one of these mindsets, we are implicitly saying that we accept it as true. On the other hand, when we notice ourselves correctly categorizing Coping mindsets as unstable, and we see ourselves rejecting the mindset, we create the possibility of consciously choosing to allow the heroic tendency to manifest itself in us.

A word of warning is needed here. It's easy to think we can easily master this process of discriminating and rejecting these Coping mindsets. We must not, however, forget just how subtle they can be and that each of them has its appealing side, designed to lure us in. Realistically, then, what you will likely find, should you determine that you want to embody the heroic principle, is that your mind will jump from one Coping mindset to another. That's because these Coping mindsets are automatic whereas Responsibility can only be entered into voluntarily. Operating from Responsibility requires first correctly identifying and refusing to operate from Coping. CA's chart becomes extremely helpful at this point.

Image 1: The Responsibility Process Poster[8]

---

8   The Responsibility Process Poster © The Responsibility Company

This work is licensed under the creative commons attribution-noderivatives 4.0 international license. To view a copy of this license, visit creativecommons.org/licenses/by-nd/4.0/

TRP®-POSTER-USA-DEC2021.PDF

A series of mental states connected together in a mostly stepwise dynamic, The Responsibility Process gets triggered by anxiety, frustration, or upset— even tiny ones. The Responsibility Process shows how we think about things that are bothering us.

– The Responsibility Process

Thanks to all the legwork we've done so far, you should already have a deep understanding of the meaning contained in the chart. With little effort, you should be able to imagine this process at work just by observing the flow represented in the chart. What's more, now that you know how this process is triggered, you know when to pause and examine your mindset, listen for the theme of the stories that you're telling yourself, discriminate between Coping and Responsibility, and ask yourself which tendency you want to embody.

Jordan B. Peterson's Christ

If you'll recall, we opened Chapter 1 with a warning that whatever JP's conception of Christ, it was bound to be complex. We spent the entire first chapter looking at JP's conception of Christ from the most fundamental level of analysis and saw how it pointed to a rather abstract and mostly mathematical process, the process that renders the Mandelbrot set visible. Then, in this chapter, we switched our level of analysis jumping to the scale that concerns human interactions or human dynamics. We used the idea of self-similarity, or symmetry across scale to illustrate how The Responsibility Process maps to the Mandelbrot set process. Having connected both of these processes to JP's conception of Christ, we now have a complete picture of what JP is pointing at when he uses the word "Christ." This complete picture consists of both the process that reveals the Mandelbrot set as well as The Responsibility Process. Both processes are the same process only operating at different scales. And like an edifice built squarely on a solid foundation, The Responsibility Process rests squarely on the Mandelbrot set process.

Christ transcends the law

We're going to bring this chapter to a close by addressing a question that many are bound to have. The question has to do with the mindset of Obligation. Obligation, more than any other Coping mindset, is easily mistaken for Responsibility. What should be immediately obvious, however, is that what is done out of Obligation cannot be said to be done voluntarily. One of the hallmarks of the heroic principle is that it can only be embodied voluntarily. So, what we see is that CA's chart truly does capture the essence of the process which Christ represents. Keeping in mind that the rule of law is a system of Obligation, consider the significance of the arrow that works its way from the bottom of CA's chart to the top. What this arrow represents is *...that spirit eternally transcends dogma, truth transcends presupposition, ... creativity updates society, and Christ transcends the law...(Beyond Order)*

TRP both looks and sounds easy, but don't be fooled. That double line that delineates between Responsibility and Coping cannot be crossed by incremental or quantitative changes. That double line represents a major paradigm shift. Responsibility constitutes a different way of thinking from Coping. Coping is instinctive and reflexive. You don't really need to think. You don't even need to be very conscious. Responsibility, on the other hand, requires volition, recognition of agency, and choice. You can just fall into a Coping mindset, but Responsibility can only be entered into voluntarily. So if you feel you have no choice, you can rest assured you haven't yet shifted from Coping to Responsibility.

> *To free yourself from the problem, you must face and examine the perceived conflict in your mind between what you have and what you want. Once you've done that, you can discover how to resolve it so you never have that particular problem again.*
>
> – The Responsibility Process

Who can believe that it is the little choices we make, every day, between good and evil, that turn the world to waste and hope to despair? But it is the case.

– Maps of Meaning

Now that JP's conception of Christ is fully visible, the process that the New Testament is a description of has been rendered spiritual (abstract and declarative); the only question is whether or not you will allow it to lead you to adopt 100% Responsibility in your life. Regardless of what you think or believe the answer to that question to be, the truth of the matter will reveal itself to you at the next upset, and the upset after that one, and so on...

The New Testament has been traditionally read as a description of a historical event, which redeemed mankind, once and for all: it might more reasonably be considered the description of a process that, if enacted, could bring about the establishment of peace on earth.

~~The problem is, however, that this process cannot yet really be said to be "consciously" – that is, explicitly – understood.~~

– Maps of Meaning

3.
REORGANIZED STRUCTURE

Transformation

The soul willing to transform, as deeply as necessary, is the most effective enemy of the demonic serpents of ideology and totalitarianism, in their personal and social forms. The healthy, dynamic, and above all else truthful personality will admit to error. It will voluntarily shed—let die—outdated perceptions, thoughts, and habits, as impediments to its further success and growth. This is the soul that will let its old beliefs burn away, often painfully, so that it can live again, and move forward, renewed. This is also the soul that will transmit what it has learned during that process of death and rebirth, so that others can be reborn along with it.

– Beyond Order

Having made JP's conception of Christ visible, we're going to consider this book's primary objective achieved. With that we can now turn our attention to making another of JP's ideas visible. The idea we're going to focus on in this chapter can be summed up with the phrase "cultural revolutionary hero." The word *cultural* is critical in this phrase. That's because the idea of the revolutionary hero is, like Christ, symmetrical across scale, and *cultural* identifies the scale we're targeting. The idea of revolutionary hero applies to problems of all sizes, which is to say, it spans, or scales, problems of all sizes. What we're interested in is the largest scale, the one that corresponds to the *bottomless abyss*, and the *ultimate monster*. And the very largest scale is the culture as a whole, which in our case is Western culture. That is, we're interested in forming a clear picture of this idea of the revolutionary hero at the scale of culture. It is precisely at that scale that *The revolutionary hero opens himself up to the possibility of advancement— to furtherance of his culture's central myth...* Just try to imagine what it might mean to further our culture's central myth, the Judeo-Christian myth, and you'll get a good enough sense of the scale that we're targeting.

As we have in the previous chapters, we are going to use JP's thinking as our guide. Only in this chapter, we're going to narrow our field of vision to a single train of thought, one that we've encountered briefly already. That train of thought has to do with the transformation of the individual soul, and the reorganizing of the hero's internal structure. In MoM, JP tells us that the *hero is the first person to have his "internal structure" reorganized.* Then, in *Beyond Order*, he informs us *that the soul willing to transform, as deeply as necessary, the soul that will let its old beliefs burn away, is also the soul that will transmit what it has learned during the process of death and rebirth.* You might be tempted to think that the previous two chapters constitute what I have learned, but that would be something like getting to the end of Chapter 1 and concluding that we could see all of what JP means by Christ. Yes, JP's conception of Christ constitutes a significant, even vital part of what I've learned, but there's something else that I've learned that is equally important. That, however, is something that can really only be *transmitted* by making the nature of this transformation itself visible.

The objective we face in this chapter, then, is similar to the challenge we faced in the previous chapters in attempting to make something as complex as JP's conception of Christ visible. This challenge is equally daunting. If, at the end of this chapter, you are able to see, to visualize precisely how my personal internal structure has been reorganized, we will have succeeded.

The Bible: The precondition for the manifestation of Truth

The most fundamental stories of the West are to be found, for better or worse, in the biblical corpus.

– Beyond Order

We're going to open ourselves up to the possibility of advancement of our culture's central myth. For this reason, we need to recognize that the thread that ties everything together, in this chapter, is the Bible. This should come as no surprise seeing as, up to this point, we've been dealing with the process that the New Testament is a description of and the New Testament cannot be divorced from the remainder of the Bible. A fitting place to start, then, is JP's thinking about the Bible starting with the idea that the Bible constitutes *the most fundamental stories of the West.* The question, of course, is what precisely does JP mean by fundamental? We'll let him answer that question:

The more ideas are dependent on a given idea, the more fundamental that idea is. That's a definition of fundamental.

So now, imagine you have an aggregation of texts in a civilization, and you say "Which are the fundamental texts?" and the answer is, the texts upon which most other texts depend. And so you put Shakespeare way in there, in English, because so many texts are dependent on Shakespeare's literary revelations. And Milton would be in that category. And Dante would be in that category, at least in translation—fundamental authors part of the Western canon—because those texts influenced more other texts. And you think of that as a hierarchy, okay, with the Bible at its base, which is certainly the case.

Now imagine that's the entire corpus of linguistic production, all things considered. Now how do you understand that? Like, literally, how do you understand that? The answer is, you sample it by reading and listening to stories and listening to people talk. You sample that whole domain and you build a low-resolution representation of that inside you and then you listen and see through that. And so, it isn't that the Bible is true. It's that the Bible is the precondition for the manifestation of truth which makes it way more true than just true. I think that is not only literally the case, factually, I think it can't be any other way. It's the only way we can solve the problem of perception.[9]

To start with, let's focus on what is arguably the most important idea being expressed in the above quote, at least as far as our purposes are concerned. That idea is that we all have a lens through which we *listen and see,* a lens through which we perceive or translate what we perceive into something meaningful. That lens has a structure, a structure that consists of an aggregation of all of the stories that we are exposed to and remember. We listen and see through this lens, which is to say we make sense of what we observe through these stories. This aggregation of stories bends what we perceive in much the same way that the cornea bends light in order to focus that light.

We're going to leverage this analogy to our advantage. We can't really see this lens, but it's easy enough to see how the stories we believe bend what we perceive out in the world in order to have it make sense, in order to bring it into focus. Even if we can't see the structure of this lens, we can comprehend its nature and understand how it works. More than that, though, we can all understand that changing the structure of this lens would result in a corresponding change to the way that what is perceived is interpreted. Anyone who's ever tried on someone else's prescription glasses understands this. This relationship between the structure of the lens and what is seen offers us a potential way forward.

There's a relationship between this lens of perception and a person's internal structure. This relationship manifests itself through the fact that any change to the lens implies a corresponding change to this internal structure. In theory, then, we should be able to picture or visualize a transformation of this structure through careful observation of changes to the lens. This

---

9   Jordan Peterson's Realization About the Bible: https://youtu.be/Vt9K6kmpx44?t=182

approach is somewhat indirect, but it should be sufficient to the task at hand: *If the axe you have in hand is sharp enough to chop down the tree then it's a good enough axe. And that's the way that we define truth pragmatically in the absence of infinite knowledge about everything.* (From Sam Harris, Jordan Peterson & Douglas Murray in Dublin - Part 3. https://youtu.be/PqpYxD71hJU?t=2514

In each chapter of my life, I operated from a different paradigm, a different point of view. We're going to explore each of these perspectives only enough to "get the picture," as it were. We're going to look at them in chronological order paying particular attention to the transformation that takes place as we move from one paradigm to the next. Each paradigm, in this way, represents the lens through which I perceived during the corresponding period in my life. Each of these lenses, in turn, can be thought of as an individual layer of a composite lens made up of all three. This composite lens, then, will represent the structure through which I currently perceive. Looking at each lens individually and then combining them in this way will serve to illustrate the nature of the reorganization of my internal structure.

The lens of perception 1: Catholic

The idea of reading a large enough sample from the entirety of the domain of Western literary production was never in the cards for me. Reading that many books simply wasn't going to happen. To a large extent, the fault was mine. What I mean by that is that I lacked the capacity and the desire to take this approach, the approach JP took. The obstacle for me was reading itself, or more precisely, the obstacle consisted of an aversion I had to reading because of how difficult I found it. It didn't help, of course, that my father was a carpenter with only a grade-six education, or that I never saw him read a book. He was a man of action, operating fully from within the forum for action way of construing the world. I observed him doing many things, but reading was not one of them.

My mother, on the other hand, was considerably more educated than my father, having graduated high school, the first in her family to do so.

Her upbringing had been rather hard, however. From the stories she told, I suspect if anyone ever read to her, it would have been the foster parents she lived with from ages four to ten. Regardless, the simple fact was that she never read to me either, so it's not hard to imagine that I never really got hooked on reading. Worse than that, reading was work to me, hard work, and for this reason, as well as other reasons I won't get into, I actively avoided it. For instance, all through high school I chose which courses I would take largely based on the amount of reading the course entailed—the more reading, the more likely I was to avoid it. I also found tricks to circumvent actually doing the assigned reading in those courses I couldn't avoid. And so, by the time I graduated high school, I had probably read no more than a couple of dozen books from any domain. I suspect this small sample size was insufficient to construct even a low-resolution representation of anything.

To correctly understand the structure of this first layer of my lens of perception, we must think of it as having been crafted by religion rather than literature. In fact, religion was baked right into the culture I was born into. Both my parents grew up in the province of Quebec (Canada) at a time when more than 90% of Quebec's population consisted of practicing Catholics. And so, in keeping with the Catholic tradition, I became a member of that culture at my baptism, shortly after my birth. Catholics waste little time getting their children baptized because the soul of a child that dies unbaptized is considered "lost" or at least doomed to a near eternity in purgatory. So, my parents took the necessary steps to ensure that my soul was safe and that I was integrated into the culture. From that point on, I was Catholic regardless of the fact that I hadn't chosen this for myself.

My parents weren't overtly religious at home. We didn't, for example, say grace before each meal and, except on occasion when I was very young, praying before going to bed wasn't a ritual we kids were expected to perform. There weren't a lot of religious symbols in our home, either. Sure, there were a few—an image of Mary in the hallway, and a crucifix or two, are all I really remember; oh, and my mother's rosary. But there was one religious object that did stand out and that was the Bible.

When I was very young, my parents kept a very large leather-bound Bible on the mantle of the fireplace. It held center stage, as it were, positioned in the most prominent place in the most used room in the house. I never saw either of my parents read this Bible, but its importance and significance were understood by the position it held in the home. It was clear to me, even as a child, that this object was significant. It was sacred, but not in a superstitious sense. The Catholics I knew tended to be a superstitious bunch, and my parents, my mother especially, was no exception. Nevertheless, they didn't treat this Bible like something I needed to be afraid of. That is, I never got the sense, from either of my parents, that this book wasn't to be touched. As a result, I felt completely free to take it down and look through its pages, though I did intuit that I had to treat it with respect when doing so.

This particular Bible was a Catholic Bible and richly illustrated with copies of grand religious paintings that served to illustrate the text. As a child, long before I learned to read, I would take the Bible down from its place of prominence and flip through its pages looking for these images, even though some of them were quite frightening, like the one of John the Baptist's head being brought to Herodias' daughter on a platter (Matthew 14: 11). These images vividly recounted the Biblical stories to my young mind without a single word. This was my introduction to the Bible. Furthermore, this book's place of honor was reinforced each week at church where it took its place on the altar at the very front of the church. At church, however, it didn't simply act as a symbol; it was read, out loud. Through these communal readings, I got to hear about the details of some of the stories that I was already familiar with through the illustrations in my parent's Bible.

My culture, the culture I grew up in, was Catholic through and through. My parents, both of them, attended church faithfully. I attended Catholic schools, where the sacraments were taught and embodied. Even in high school, mass would be held on holy days or during the most significant periods of the religious calendar such as lent and advent. I acted out these rituals always with an implicit belief that they found their origin within this most holy of books. My parent's Bible and the Catholic culture—with its ceremonies, rituals, and sermons—all served to inform me about these most fundamental of stories. This is how the first layer of my lens of perception was constructed, and the stories from which it was built. It's safe to say, then, that the most fundamental stories of the West comprised the majority of the stories aggregated into the low-resolution representation that is this first lens.

First death and rebirth

Movement from Catholic to Protestant constitutes the sort of *movement from one schema to another* that we looked at in the previous chapter. There we saw that this type of movement *presupposes dissolution... not mere addition (presupposes a "qualitative" shift, not a "quantitative" shift)*. What this means is that the path from Catholic to Protestant isn't linear or gradual (i.e., quantitative) but discontinuous (i.e., qualitative). There's a chasm that separates the two and the crossing of this chasm constitutes the very sort of death and rebirth that JP talks about.

The movement from Catholic to Protestant constitutes a change in point of view. It's a move from a primarily implicit symbolic and imagistic system to a more abstract and explicitly declared system of belief. What's hard to see, if you don't have personal experience with these two systems of belief, is that they are entirely incompatible. That is, they constitute paradigms founded on entirely different axioms. For this reason, the transformation from Catholic to evangelical involved abandoning the axioms of the Catholic faith and adopting the axioms of the Protestant faith. The Protestant faith is more explicit and its axioms are stated very clearly in the five Solas, the five pillars of the Protestant Reformation. These five Solas state that salvation is one, by grace alone (Sola Gratia); two, through faith alone (Sola Fide); three, in Christ alone (Solus Christus); four, as revealed by Scripture alone (Sola Scriptura); and finally, all of this is to the glory of God alone (Soli Deo Gloria). These are the axioms upon which the Protestant faith rests and the foundation upon which I would find myself standing once the transformation from Catholic to Protestant had fully played out. I would stand on this foundation for the duration of my apprenticeship.

Transformations of this sort—the kind that requires movement from one paradigm to another, the kind that requires a death of the existing point of view and the adoption of a new one—don't just happen. There needs to be sufficient reason for crossing that chasm. For me, the motivation was two-fold. The first started while still a Catholic and, stated very simply, it boiled down to a lack of meaning. I went looking for answers within the Catholic system but couldn't find them there. For instance, I once asked our priest what exactly was meant by the expression "Christ died for our sins." As a Catholic, I mouthed those words every week but the meaning, the specific meaning of that phrase, eluded me as if it were shrouded in a fog of mystery. In asking this question, I discovered that it hadn't only eluded me but the priest as well. All of the answers within the Catholic system seemed to boil down to "mystery." Mystery seemed to be the answer to all of the hard questions, and this didn't sit well with me. My mind, my intellect couldn't buy into this, and so my attachment to my culture's faith remained weak, too weak to keep me afloat when I stepped out of my parent's home and into the world.

To say that I was unprepared when I left home, at nineteen, with just a high school education doesn't do it justice. The world changed while I was in high school and the economy tanked just as I was stepping out into that world. On top of that, I behaved like a fool and jumped right into the deep end before making sure I could even swim. By twenty-one, I was doing my best trying to cope with the responsibilities of a wife and a newborn while also dealing with the reality of mortality as my mother was in the final stages of losing her battle with cancer. I was completely overwhelmed. I'd jumped without looking, and now I felt like the world was going to crush me alive.

When things seemed completely unbearable, hope came knocking, in the form of a book. The story of how I came to buy my first Bible is of the sort that makes us use words like "fate" and "destiny" and "providence." We aren't going to get into the details, however. We'll leave it at, I was drowning, going under for the third time, and just then an encounter with a man who sold me a Bible altered the trajectory of my miserable life. The Bible I could have gotten anywhere. What mattered, what made the difference, is the man who sold it to me. He was trying to sell me something, no doubt about it, but I could sense that he was genuinely concerned for my wellbeing and he honestly believed the Bible could help. He even went so far as to give me a bit of advice on how to approach the Bible. He suggested that I start with Proverbs, Psalms, and the Gospels, and once I was familiar enough with those books, to expand my reading, first to the rest of the New Testament and finally the rest of the Old Testament. I followed his advice and soon found myself being comforted by David, mentored by Solomon, and called by Christ.

While it's not literally true to say that I learned to read by reading the Bible, the truth isn't very far from this. I wasn't exactly illiterate when I started reading the Bible, but you'd never guess it to watch me back then. I would sit there, Bible in one hand, dictionary in the other. At first, it felt like I couldn't get through a verse without having to look up the meaning of some word that I either didn't know or I was fuzzy about. Often, I'd have to look up the meaning of the words within the definition as well; my vocabulary was just so underdeveloped at the time. My attitude towards reading meant that I'd barely developed the skill so I literally felt like I learned to read when I started reading the Bible. Only now I had something I hadn't had before. Now I had something motivating me. The Bible spoke to me, and putting the Bible into practice helped me get my life in order, and so reading the Bible came with its own rewards.

The words I read called out to me and I found myself responding positively to that call. This was not an academic exercise for me. I didn't study the Bible simply to know about the Bible. No, having grown up in the world as forum for action, my interest was fundamentally pragmatic. So I developed the practice of reading the Bible regularly. Within a few years this practice evolved into a disciplined habit. I orbited the New Testament, Psalms, and Proverbs as the moon orbits the earth and the Old Testament as the earth orbits the sun. It was precisely through reading the Bible that

I began to *apprehend what is of value*, and *what we should aim* at in exactly the way that JP describes in *Beyond Order*:

> *Question: Who are you—or, at least, who could you be? Answer: Part of the eternal force that constantly confronts the terrible unknown, voluntarily; part of the eternal force that transcends naivete and becomes dangerous enough, in a controlled manner, to understand evil and beard it in its lair; and part of the eternal force that faces chaos and turns it into productive order, or that takes order that has become too restrictive, reduces it to chaos, and renders it productive once again.*
>
> *And all of this, being very difficult to understand consciously but vital to our survival, is transmitted in the form of the stories that we cannot help but attend to. And it is in this manner that we come to apprehend what is of value, what we should aim at, and what we could be.*
>
> *– Beyond Order*

It's in this way that the day I began reading the Bible turned out to be the day that my nearly two-decade long apprenticeship to Christ, to The Master, began.

The lens of perception 2: evangelical fundamentalist

> *In sterquiliniis invenitur—in filth it will be found.*
>
> *– Maps of Meaning*

> *After much searching, Harry gains entrance to this underworld labyrinth of pipes and tunnels, and finds the central chamber. He does this, significantly, through the sewer, acting out the ancient alchemical dictum, in sterquilinis invenitur: in filth it will be found.*
>
> *– Beyond Order*

*Furthermore, fundamentalists are bound by a relationship with
the transcendent. What this means is that God, the center of their
moral universe, remains outside and above complete understanding, according to the fundamentalist's own creed.*

– *Beyond Order*

Our journey, at this point, leads down into the filth that is fundamentalist
dogma to JP. This is unavoidable if we're to develop a picture of the second
layer of the composite lens of perception that we are building. Doing so will
forming a clear enough idea of what precisely it means to be a fundamentalist
evangelical Christian. More than that, however, we're interested in seeing
how a fundamentalist Christian measures up to JP's ideas. From what I've
heard come out of JP's mouth, I've gotten the distinct impression that he's not
much of a fan. You catch a glimpse of this in *Beyond Order* when he puts the
fundamentalist in the same general category as the ideologue. *Ideologues are
the intellectual equivalent of fundamentalists, unyielding and rigid.* He doesn't
seem to want to see the fundamentalist as an apprentice even though his
words suggest that he should. *Initially, the apprentice must become a servant
of tradition, of structure, and of dogma (Beyond Order). Doesn't this suggest
that the fundamentalist is simply an apprentice serving dogma, imitat-
ing Christ's example? Psychologically speaking, Christ is a representation,
or an embodiment, of the mastery of dogma and the (consequent) emergence
of spirit (Beyond Order).*

Let's see how the evangelical faith stacks up against JP's ideas of what
a true believer, a true Christian, should look like. The following two quotes
from MoM are representative of his thinking.

*The significance of the Christian passion is the transformation
of the process by which the goal is to be attained, into the goal
itself: the making of the "imitation of Christ"—the duty of every
Christian citizen, so to speak—into the embodiment of coura-
geous, truthful individually unique existence...*

Alchemy was a living myth: the myth of the individual man, as redeemer. Organized Christianity had "sterilized itself," so to speak, by insisting on the worship of something external as the means to salvation. The alchemists (re)discovered the error of this presumption, and came to realize that identification with the redeemer was in fact necessary, not his "worship" – came to realize that myths of redemption had true power when they were "incorporated," and acted out, rather than "believed" in some abstract sense. This meant: to say that Christ was "the greatest man in history" —a combination of the divine and mortal—was not sufficient "expression of faith." Sufficient expression meant, alternatively, the attempt to live out the myth of the hero within the confines of individual personality to voluntarily shoulder the cross of existence, to "unite the opposites" within a single breast, and to serve as active conscious mediator between the eternal generative forces of known and unknown.

Let's see how these ideas compare to evangelical Christianity. I thought, for this purpose, it would be fitting to turn to one of the most influential books of my early Christian life. The book is J. I. Packer's *Knowing God*. This book, a Christian classic, is representative of the Christianity that I adhered to. Packer's *Knowing God* was instrumental in pointing me in the right direction early in my journey, and his *Quest for Godliness* guided me into the depths of the Christian faith. Packer's voice is solidly mainstream evangelical. His thinking, his ideas, can therefore serve as a measure against which to gauge or evaluate the degree to which JP's ideas align with evangelical thinking. So let's turn our attention to *Knowing God* to get us started:

In A Preface to Christian Theology, John Mackay illustrated two kinds of interest in Christian things by picturing persons sitting on the high front balcony of a Spanish house watching travelers go by on the road below. The "balconeers" can overhear the travelers' talk and chat with them; they may comment critically on the way that the travelers walk; or they may discuss questions about the road, how it can exist at all or lead anywhere, but they are onlookers, and their problems are theoretical only. The travelers, by contrast, face problems which, though they have their theoretical angle, are essentially practical—problems of the "which-way-to-go" and "how-to-make-it" type, problems which call not merely for comprehension but for decision and action too. Balconeers and travelers may think over the same area, yet their problems differ. Thus (for instance) in relation to evil, the balconeer's problem, is to find a theoretical explanation of how evil can consist with God's sovereignty and goodness, but the travelers' problem is how to master evil and bring good out of it.

– Knowing God

The evangelical Christian, if he is so in reality and not just in name, is the traveler in this analogy. The traveler is focused on the idea expressed by JP as *the attempt to live out the myth of the hero [Christ] within the confines of individual personality.* The traveler represents the individual who has answered the call to adventure. Packer's *Knowing God* is a book for travelers, for those actively following the call. As a result, a careful reading of *Knowing God* will reveal that the ideas in it run parallel with JP's thinking. In fact, if you make Packer's "God" equivalent to JP's "Highest Good," you find the same ideas being expressed in nearly the same words.

Consider for a moment that JP tells us, in *Beyond Order*, that "You are possessed of an instinct—a spirit—that orients you toward the highest good." Let's see how Packer communicates the same idea, keeping in mind that he is telling us what the Bible teaches—what the Bible, the most fundamental of stories in the West, tells us to value and aim at:

What were we made for? To know God.

What aim should we set ourselves in life? To know God.

What is the "eternal life" that Jesus gives? Knowledge of God. "This is eternal life: that they may know you, the only true God, and Jesus Christ, whom you have sent" (Jn 17:3).

What is the best thing in life, bringing more joy, delight and contentment than anything else? Knowledge of God. This is what the LORD says: "Let not the wise man boast of his wisdom or the strong man boast of his strength or the rich man boast of his riches, but let him who boasts boast about this: that he understands and knows me" (Jer 9:23-24).

What, of all the states God ever sees man in, gives God most pleasure? Knowledge of himself. "I desired ... the knowledge of God more than burnt offerings," says God (Hos 6:6 KJV).

– Knowing God

It stands to reason that if we are possessed of an instinct that orients us toward the highest good, we must be made to know God. These ideas are interchangeable. But is the evangelical idea of knowing God equivalent to *the attempt to live out the myth of the hero within the confines of individual personality,* or is it the same *sterilized* Christianity that prompted the alchemists to go deeper? We've already suggested that it's the former. The balconeer, for example, represents a sterilized interest in religion while the traveler is busy living out the myth within his own life. But the point is so vital, so critical, that we're going to want something more than just an analogy.

What is of value and what we should aim at

Our aim in studying the Godhead must be to know God himself better. Our concern must be to enlarge our acquaintance, not simply with the doctrine of God's attributes, but with the living God whose attributes they are. As he is the subject of our study, and our helper in it, so he must himself be the end of it. We must seek, in studying God, to be led to God. It was for this purpose that revelation was given, and it is to this use that we must put it.

– Knowing God

The fundamentalist is *bound by a relationship with the transcendent,* his God. What's more, to the fundamentalist, one of the defining attributes of God is that He is good. This is obviously equivalent to the highest good. That's what we should value and aim at. But what about dogma? For JP, *the true "believer" rises above dogmatic adherence to realize the soul of the hero—to "incarnate that soul"—in every aspect of their day-to-day life (MoM).* There are two aspects to this. First, there is the *rising above dogma* element and then there's the day-to-day living out or *incarnation* of the *soul of the hero,* which is to say the embodying of Christ. Before turning to Packer, let's pause to consider something that JP seems to have missed with respect to this rising above dogma.

Rising above is not the circumvention of but a mastery of dogma. The distinction is critical. After all, *psychologically speaking, Christ is a representation, or an embodiment, of the mastery of dogma.* Mastery, however, requires a prolonged period, generally at least 10,000 hours of "practice," of "religious" adherence first. Apprenticeship, therefore, is the only valid path to this sort of rising above. *Apprenticeship means heat and pressure... The goal of this heat and pressure is subordination of an undeveloped personality (by no means "individual" at this point) to a single path, for the purposes of transformation from undisciplined beginner to accomplished master (Beyond Order).* What this means is that we should assume that most evangelicals are in the apprenticeship stage of their journey, the stage in which they are still subordinating themselves to dogma and are not yet masters. These apprentices will obviously appear *unyielding and rigid* as they serve dogma, but it must be remembered that they, at least, are on the road to its mastery.

Having said that, let's look at the evangelical attitude toward dogma or, what Christians call doctrine:

*As we saw earlier, there can be no spiritual health without doctri-
nal knowledge; but it is equally true that there can be no spiritual
health with it, if it is sought for the wrong purpose and valued
by the wrong standard. In this way, doctrinal study really can
become a danger to spiritual life, and we today, no less than the
Corinthians of old, need to be on our guard here.*

– Knowing God

Here we see a reflection of JP's thinking. Dogma, doctrinal knowledge,
is necessary but requires proper handling. Packer warns his reader of the
danger of doctrinal knowledge of the type that makes doctrine or dogma
an end in itself rather than a means to an end. The truly *unyielding and rigid*
individual is valuing the wrong thing. He has failed to learn the first lesson
concerning what we should value most. So we see that Packer recognizes the
threat of conflating knowledge about God with knowledge of God. Knowing
about God is necessary but, ultimately, empty if it isn't accompanied by
knowledge of God. That brings us to our second point, that of incarnating
the soul of the hero.

Let's go back to what constitutes *sufficient expression of faith* in JP's
thinking. JP uses the alchemist's ideas as a standard of what such a thing
would look like. He tells us that the alchemists *came to realize that identification with the redeemer was in fact necessary"* (MoM) and that *sufficient
expression* meant *the attempt to live out the myth of the hero within the confines of individual personality—to voluntarily shoulder the cross of existence,
to "unite the opposites" within a single breast, and to serve as active conscious
mediator between the eternal generative forces of known and unknown.* Let's
turn to Packer again to see how his conception of knowing God, the evangelical conception of knowing God, compares:

*First, knowing God is a matter of personal dealing, as is all direct
acquaintance with personal beings. Knowing God is more than
knowing about him; it is a matter of dealing with him as he opens
up to you, and being dealt with by him as he takes knowledge of*

you. Knowing about him is a necessary precondition of trusting in him ("how could they have faith in one they had never heard of?" [Rom 10:14 NEB]), but the width of our knowledge about him is no gauge of the depth of our knowledge of him...

Second, knowing God is a matter of personal involvement—mind, will and feeling. It would not, indeed, be a fully personal relationship otherwise. To get to know another person, you have to commit yourself to his company and interests, and be ready to identify yourself with his concerns. Without this, your relationship with him can only be superficial and flavorless. "Taste and see that the LORD is good," says the psalmist (Ps 34:8). To "taste" is, as we say, to "try" a mouthful of something, with a view to appreciating its flavor. A dish may look good, and be well recommended by the cook, but we do not know its real quality till we have tasted it.

Similarly, we do not know another person's real quality till we have "tasted" the experience of friendship...

Third, knowing God is a matter of grace. It is a relationship in which the initiative throughout is with God—as it must be, since God is so completely above us and we have so completely forfeited all claim on his favor by our sins. We do not make friends with God; God makes friends with us, bringing us to know him by making his love known to us. Paul expresses this thought of the priority of grace in our knowledge of God when he writes to the Galatians, "Now that you know God-or rather are known by God" (Gal 4:9).

... knowing God involves, first, listening to God's Word and receiving it as the Holy Spirit interprets it, in application to oneself; second, noting God's nature and character, as his Word and works reveal it; third, accepting his invitations and doing what he commands; fourth, recognizing and rejoicing in the love that

he has shown in thus approaching you and drawing you into this divine fellowship.

The Bible puts flesh on these bare bones of ideas by using pictures and analogies. It tells us that we know God in the manner of a son knowing his father, a wife knowing her husband, a subject knowing his king and a sheep knowing its shepherd (these are the four main analogies employed). All four analogies point to a relation in which the knower "looks up" to the one known, and the latter takes responsibility for the welfare of the former. This is part of the biblical concept of knowing God, that those who know him—that is, those by whom he allows himself to be known—are loved and cared for by him...

Then the Bible adds the further point that we know God in this way only through knowing Jesus Christ

– Knowing God

I trust that it's obvious that Packer's description of what knowing God means constitutes genuine *identification with the redeemer even by JP's standards.* Packer is representative of the Christianity that I followed for nearly two decades. This was the nature of my apprenticeship, my discipleship. I had gone all-in and throughout this second chapter I fully intended and expected to live out the remainder of my life as an evangelical. But God, as they say, had other plans.

Second death: the death of God

Movement from the Catholic to the Protestant worldview, like movement from one paradigm, or schema, to another, required the dissolution of the old to adopt the new. That is, the transformation from Catholic to Protestant involved wiping the slate clean and starting over from scratch as it were. The only thing that remained during the first *death and rebirth* paradigm shift was the very foundation, God. Everything else had to be re-evaluated and all things that did not conform to sound Biblical doctrine discarded.

And, in the end, all that remained once this process was complete was the foundation. This may not sound like a big deal, but the transformation was extreme, dramatic, and far-reaching. Nevertheless, the magnitude of this change pales in comparison to the second *death and rebirth* transformation because, in this case, nothing remained, not even the foundation.

Each chapter of my life was lived from within a particular paradigm or worldview. Movement forward, from one chapter to the next, involved letting my old beliefs die as I moved from the worldview in the previous chapter to the one that would dominate in the next. The third chapter in my life was one in which God no longer played a part. That is precisely what walking away from God entailed. There's an idea that JP brings to light in various places that is extremely relevant to this transition, and that idea is captured in Nietzsche's proclamation that God is dead. JP elaborates on this idea of the death of God in *12 Rules for Life* like this:

> *Carl Jung continued to develop Nietzsche's arguments decades later, pointing out that Europe awoke, during the Enlightenment, as if from a Christian dream, noticing that everything it had heretofore taken for granted could and should be questioned. "God is dead," said Nietzsche. "God remains dead. And we have killed him. How shall we, murderers of all murderers, console ourselves? That which was the holiest and mightiest of all that the world has yet possessed has bled to death under our knives. Who will wipe this blood off us?"*

The idea that *Europe awoke...as if from a Christian dream* captures the essence of this transformation. Within a very short time, once I'd committed to this direction, I experienced something like this waking up from a *Christian dream*. To appreciate the nature of this waking up, we need to understand this *death of God* idea a bit better and there's one insight JP provides in MoM that is particularly significant:

*The fictional characters of Shakespeare and Dostoevsky respond
like the flesh-and-blood man, Tolstoy, to the same historically
determined set of circumstances—to the "death of god," in
Nietzsche's terminology, brought about, inexorably, by continued
development of abstract consciousness.*

Here JP tells us that the death of God was brought on by the *continued development of abstract consciousness*. What's more, JP tells us that the development of abstract consciousness marches inexorably, that is, in a way that is impossible to stop or prevent, towards the death of God. We see then, that there is a sort of threshold along the developmental path where abstract consciousness becomes incompatible with God, or at least the Western conception of God. And, without knowing it, I had been steadily marching down this developmental path at my own pace. As a Catholic, my worldview was rather concrete. I wasn't concerned with abstract ideas unless I could see how they applied to the real world. The transition to the Protestant faith was a step into more abstract thinking. In the first chapter of my life, books played a nearly insignificant role. The second chapter, however, was filled with books. Nevertheless, as a fundamentalist working in a job that didn't require further development of abstract thought, I managed to live below what might be called the "lethal" threshold of abstract consciousness. I lived below this threshold but marched steadily towards it. Then, in the last three and a half years of the second chapter of my life, I embarked on a course of action that took me beyond that threshold. The course of action? Going back to school to get my degree in computer engineering. The outcome? My very own personal experience of the death of God.

My experience of the death of God was triggered by approximately the *same historically-determined set of circumstances* that converged on Tolstoy, only in my case, those circumstances materialized more than a hundred years later. While the timing was different, the experience was virtually the same. With the death of God came the death of purpose, meaning, hope. This was something I hadn't anticipated. I didn't know, when I walked away from God, that I was experiencing this *death of God*, that I was taking my part with the *murderers of all murderers,* and I certainly didn't know that I was diving into an abyss. All I knew was that I was stepping out into the unknown and I was doing so with both feet, so to speak. Nevertheless, with that "step" I jumped in, or perhaps, more accurately, dove in. I didn't realize it at first, but I'd moved off from solid ground and began to sink, slowly, steadily, until one day, about five years later, Bible verses stopped coming to mind. At this point, my old conception of God was, in very fact dead and I had consciously and deliberately killed Him. The very notion of God was now something like a dream I'd woken up from. God became a rationalized fiction I knew I had once believed but could no longer comprehend how, because I could no longer conceive of God as I once had. And, of course, along with the death of God came the death of all sense of meaning and purpose. And so there I was, swallowed up by the monster at the bottom of that abyss:

> *Social and biological conditions define the boundaries of individual existence. The unfailing pursuit of interest provides the subjective means by which these conditions can be met, and their boundaries transcended. Meaning is the instinct that makes life possible. When it is abandoned, individuality loses its redeeming power. The great lie is that meaning does not exist, or that it is not important. When meaning is denied, hatred for life and the wish for its destruction inevitably rules.*

– Maps of Meaning

The great lie! Meaning does not exist! As I mentioned in the previous chapter, what JP says about Nietzsche in *Beyond Order* could have been said about me at this time: *Nietzsche appears to have unquestioningly adopted the idea that the world was both objective and valueless in the manner posited by the emergent physical sciences.* I simply did not, could not believe that purpose, in any objective sense, existed. Purpose and meaning became just pleasant stories we told ourselves to make life bearable. That was my official position on the matter. Then, once purpose and meaning had fully been erased from the list of things I believed in, hopelessness, despair, and depression became my constant companions. They would remain my companions for years. I had jumped headlong into the bottomless abyss and been devoured whole by the ultimate monster that lurks in the depths of that nihilistic pit.

Another rebirth

For the first few years after walking away from God, I stopped reading altogether. In order to cope with the depression, I decided to pick up the habit again, only this time I found myself drawn to audiobooks, which allowed me to exercise at the same time. I'd never been much a fan of fiction and that wasn't going to change. I was interested in things that expanded my understanding and now that I was no longer constrained by religious thinking and no longer having any belief system to protect, I was free to follow my interest wherever it lead. I explored, for example, the question of how old the universe is and how we know this. I explored what we know about evolution and, more importantly, genesis or the emergence of life. I explored in a rather haphazard way, jumping here and there as it suited me. I had no plan but followed a seemingly random path of exploration.

As ironic as this is going to sound, I've never been interested in mythology. As a Christian, the Bible had not been a myth but the Word of God. As a result, I knew nothing of the hero myth or the idea of the revolutionary hero but in hindsight, I can see that my interests lead me to explore the great revolutionary heroes in the domain of physics. As a Christian, I'd been drawn to stories of great Christians, and in a similar manner, I now found myself drawn to stories of great scientists and scientific breakthroughs. Interestingly enough, in a very abstract way, I was still motivated to seek God. God is light (1 John 1:5), and I was drawn to one revolutionary hero in particular for whom light played a particularly significant role: Albert Einstein. In Einstein, I found someone who embodied the spirit of the heroic, and I was attracted to that. What's more, Einstein's most significant breakthroughs, his theories of special and general relativity, were inextricably linked to the nature and behavior of light. Many of his thought experiments, for instance, shed light on the nature of light itself. As a result, I found myself captivated by just how strange a thing light actually is

Everywhere I explored, I gained deeper insights into this very strange thing that we all take for granted. The more I explored, the more it became apparent just how significant a role light played in the revolutionary transformation that took place in physics at the turn of the twentieth century. Max Planck laid the foundation for quantum physics with his discovery of the quanta while studying black body radiation, *a term used to describe the relationship between an object's temperature, and the wavelength of electromagnetic radiation it emits.* Electromagnetic radiation, that's light. That was in 1900; then in 1905, Einstein used the fact that light travels at a constant speed, to produce his paper on special relativity, the paper that includes the now famous equation, $E = mc2$. There are probably few things as vitally important to our existence as light. Like the air that we breathe, we take light for granted, but light has a lot to teach us about the nature of reality.

Many of the books I listened to described the classic double-slit experiment that allows us to "see" the dual nature of light. Some of the books, however, provided details of more elaborate double-slit experiments in which scientists played around with the configuration of the experiment in very creative ways. They might, for instance, turn on a photon detector only after the photon had passed some point along its path. What these experiments reveal about light provides a window into the strange world that exists at the smallest of scales; provides a window into the quantum world. Who would have guessed that light behaves differently when it's being observed than it does when it's not. That is, once we have information about which path a photon took in a double-slit experiment, then what we invariably find is that light behaves as if it's a particle; otherwise it acts like a wave. Light then, behaves as if it is aware of the fact that it's being watched. Or, stated another way, light acts in such a way as to draw attention to consciousness. Light, as it turns out, behaves in a completely counterintuitive manner and it's only through abstract consciousness that we know this.

The point I'm trying to make is that, unlike the first transformation, the one that moved me from the Catholic to the Protestant paradigm, this transformation took a lot longer precisely because it left me with no foundation on which to stand. I didn't realize it at the time, but what I was doing was slowly laying an entirely new foundation. For me, that foundation was physics, and more precisely, the pillars of physics. As I've already alluded to, Einstein's relativity and quantum mechanics constitute two of these pillars. But there's a third pillar in physics, and learning about this one played a critical part in allowing me to see JP's conception of Christ. That third pillar, if you haven't guessed, is chaos:

> *IN THE HEADY early days, researchers described chaos as the century's third revolution in the physical sciences, after relativity and quantum mechanics. What has become clear now is that chaos is inextricable from relativity and quantum mechanics. There is only one physics.*
>
> *– Chaos*

In hindsight, I can see that I'd followed my interest and it had lead me to explore the boundary between the known and the unknown, with the twentieth century's three revolutions in the physical sciences defining the limits of that boundary. Quantum physics defines what we know about the nature of reality at the smallest of scales. Relativity does the same thing for reality at the very largest of scales. And chaos deals with the scale at which we live:

> *The most passionate advocates of the new science go so far as to say that twentieth-century science will be remembered for just three things: relativity, quantum mechanics, and chaos. Chaos, they contend, has become the century's third great revolution in the physical sciences. Like the first two revolutions, chaos cuts*

away at the tenets of Newton's physics... Of the three, the revolution in chaos applies to the universe we see and touch, to objects at human scale.

– Chaos

Culture has become permeated with many terms from these three revolutions even though few have any idea of what those terms really mean. Relativity, for instance, often conjures up the idea that everything is relative. What is rarely understood, however, is that while Einstein's framework does reveal that the axioms of Newtonian physics, absolute time and absolute space, were wrong, it replaces these with its own axiom of absolute space-time, which resolves the apparent contradictions created by relative space and time. So Einstein didn't get rid of absolutes but merely discovered that what was absolute was a level of abstraction deeper than previously thought. One of the central ideas in chaos has also been integrated into culture in this way. That idea is the butterfly effect. This term, like relativity, is well known and little understood. Few people familiar with the term, for instance, have any idea that the butterfly effect is a term that describes systems, non-linear dynamical systems, systems that display sensitive dependence on initial conditions. While these terms have been integrated into the culture, an understanding of the terms hasn't been.

Before moving on, then, it's worth highlighting what is arguably the greatest insight to come out of this third revolution in the physical sciences. If we ask ourselves, what exactly was the nature of this revolution, we find that the answer has to do with the nature of complexity and the overturning of our intuitions about complexity. As it turns out, our thinking was completely upside down, and the revolution in chaos, turned our thinking right-side up. Here's how Gleick summarizes the most significant aspect of this revolution:

TWO DECADES AGO Edward Lorenz was thinking about the atmosphere, Michel Hénon the stars, Robert May the balance of nature. Benoit Mandelbrot was an unknown IBM mathematician,

Mitchell Feigenbaum an undergraduate at the City College of New York, Doyne Farmer a boy growing up in New Mexico. Most practicing scientists shared a set of beliefs about complexity. They held these beliefs so closely that they did not need to put them into words. Only later did it become possible to say what these beliefs were and to bring them out for examination.

Simple systems behave in simple ways. A mechanical contraption like a pendulum, a small electrical circuit, an idealized population of fish in a pond— as long as these systems could be reduced to a few perfectly understood, perfectly deterministic laws, their long term behavior would be stable and predictable.

Complex behavior implies complex causes. A mechanical device, an electrical circuit, a wildlife population, a fluid flow, a biological organ, a particle beam, an atmospheric storm, a national economy—a system that was visibly unstable, unpredictable, or out of control must either be governed by a multitude of independent components or subject to random external influences.

Different systems behave differently. A neurobiologist who spent a career studying the chemistry of the human neuron without learning anything about memory or perception, an aircraft designer who used wind tunnels to solve aerodynamic problems without understanding the mathematics of turbulence, an economist who analyzed the psychology of purchasing decisions without gaining an ability to forecast large-scale trends—scientists like these, knowing that the components of their disciplines were different, took it for granted that the complex systems made up of billions of these components must also be different.

Now all that has changed. In the intervening twenty years, physicists, mathematicians, biologists, and astronomers have created an alternative set of ideas. Simple systems give rise to complex behavior. Complex systems give rise to simple behavior. And most important, the laws of complexity hold universally, caring not at all for the details of a system's constituent atoms.

– Chaos

The central idea here is worth repeating. We used to believe that *simple systems behave in simple ways* and that *complex behavior implies complex causes* but now, on this side of this revolution, we understand that *Simple systems give rise to complex behavior. Complex systems give rise to simple behavior.* The process that reveals the Mandelbrot set is a case in point. The process itself is as simple as they come and yet it produces the most complex mathematical object in existence. Simple processes with feedback mechanisms are the stuff of LIFE, the stuff of reality, as it is, rather than as we imagine it should be.

"Evolution is chaos with feedback," Joseph Ford said. The universe is randomness and dissipation, yes. But randomness with direction can produce surprising complexity. And as Lorenz discovered so long ago, dissipation is an agent of order.

– Chaos

We've barely skimmed the surface of what amounts to the structure of the lens through which I perceived reality during this third chapter in my life. Nevertheless, the salient point is clear. When I walked away from God, I left all my evangelical ideas behind, wiped the slate completely clean, including the very foundation. I then became familiar with and adopted what can only be considered a completely modern, which is to say scientific, worldview. This transition, a transition from the world as forum for action to the world as place of things, started with the expansion of my abstract consciousness that occurred as a result of pursuing my degree. This resulted in a personal experience of the death of God and the adoption of the world as place of things worldview. The result of this multi-year process is the low-resolution representation that constitutes the third layer of my lens of perception, and the stories that this lens is an aggregation of consist largely of the greatest stories of our time, the stories of the revolutions in the physical sciences that took place in the twentieth century.

The composite lens of perception

Each chapter of my life corresponds to a different way of looking at the world, a different worldview or paradigm, a lens with a particular structure through which I made sense of the world. We've been examining each lens, getting a sense of its structure and an idea of what moving from one lens (or schema) to another would produce. To that end, we spent time examining the transition from one chapter to the next. And, having looked at the individual parts, the separate layers, we're now going to illustrate each layer and attempt to show how they fit together to form a composite lens. This exercise should leave you with a clear enough picture of the way in which my internal structure has been reorganized, the objective of this chapter.

In 2012, after having spent five years sinking to the bottom of the abyss and another three in the belly of the monster that lurks at the bottom of the nihilistic void, I ran into CA. The event marked the turning point as I recognized the equivalent of "my dead father" there, inside the monster. This discovery of *my dead father* in form of The Responsibility Process signaled the end of what JP calls a successful descent:

> *The individual troubled by anomalous and anxiety-provoking experiential data is suffering equally from the "disintegration," "rigidity" or "senility" of the society within. The choice to "process" such data—that is, to "mine" it for significance, and to destabilize the socially-constructed intrapsychic hierarchy of behavior and values, in consequence—is equivalent, mythologically speaking, to the "descent to the underworld." If this descent is successful—that is, if the exploring individual does not retreat to his previous personality structure, and wall himself in, and if he does not fall prey to hopelessness, anxiety and despair—then he may "return" to the*

community, treasure in hand, with processed information whose incorporation would benefit the remaining members of society.

– Maps of Meaning

The next stage of the journey, the ascent back to the surface, is something JP doesn't talk much about. He certainly doesn't stress the fact that the ascent is, in many ways, the most arduous part of the journey. For me, the beginning of this ascent was punctuated, appropriately enough, with a trip to Rome and, more specifically, to the Vatican. Looking back I can see just how appropriate it was that the ascent should begin with what amounts to a symbolic journey back to the first chapter of my life. Nevertheless, when I found myself standing in the Stanza della Segnatura ("Room of the Segnatura"), I failed to recognize that this room contained a symbolic representation of my life's journey. Here's how the Vatican describes the frescoes that adorn the four walls of this room:

> *The frescoed walls represent the major masterpieces personally painted by the young master from Urbino—The Dispute on the Blessed Sacrament and the School of Athens—exalting revealed Truth and natural Truth. The concept of Beauty, inspired by poetry is depicted in the Mount Parnassus fresco. Good is pictorially represented in the Theological and Cardinal Virtues and in Law...*
>
> *Raphael rejected abstractions, symbols, and allegories in pictorially interpreting the universal concepts of Truth, Beauty, and Good; instead, his creative and innovative genius seized upon "illustrious personalities" who, in the flesh give movement, light, color, and life to the philosophical content of these abstract concepts.*

– Michelangelo and Raphael in the Vatican

Truth, Beauty, and Good

Let's pause to consider the two masterpieces that represent truth, The Dispute on the Blessed Sacrament and the School of Athens. We are told that both of these works of art depict truth. The former, The Dispute as we'll call it, represents revealed truth. For anyone unfamiliar with the term, revealed truth refers to divinely revealed truth which is synonymous with Scripture or the Bible. The School of Athens also represents truth, only in this case, the truth in question is natural truth or truth that is revealed through the natural or created order. What's more, revealed truth and natural truth are depicted opposite each other, facing each other and in contradistinction to each other. This description should bring to mind something we saw in the previous chapter.

> *The central scientific axiom left to us by the Enlightenment—that reality is the exclusive domain of the objective—poses a fatal challenge to the reality of religious experience, if the latter experience is fundamentally subjective (and it appears to be exactly that).*
>
> – Beyond Order

I hope the connection between JP's two modes of construing the world and Raphael's two masterpieces, The Dispute and the School of Athens, is obvious. Recall that the nature of the problem JP has been contending with is captured in the idea that *The world can be validly construed as forum for action, or as place of things.* The world as forum for action, JP informed us, corresponds to what we could call the religious way of construing the world or the *fundamentally subjective* worldview. The world as place of things constitutes the *domain of the objective*, or scientific worldview since it *finds its formal expression in the methods and theories of science.* The problem, as we saw, lies in the fact that *No complete world-picture can be generated, without use of both modes of construal.* Unfortunately, forming such a *complete world-picture* from these two different modes of construal is further complicated by the fact that *one mode is generally set at odds with the other.* These ideas, the two modes of construing the world and the apparent conflict between the two, are captured imagistically by these two frescoes. Even their being *set at odds* is represented in this room. Standing in that room, you can't look at both at the same time. Observing one literally requires turning your back on the other.

The connection between these two frescoes and the chapters in my life should be equally as obvious. God is the central axiom of the religious point of view and The Dispute reflects this. The Dispute, therefore, makes the perfect illustration of the low-resolution representation that was the lens through which I perceived during the first chapter of my life. The School of Athens, in the same way, is the ideal illustration for the structure of the lens through which I perceived during the third chapter of my life. My entire life's journey can be illustrated using this room and a simple analogy.

Imagine standing at the center of the Room of the Signatura and being captivated by The Dispute, or religious point of view, for forty years. Then, imagine doing an about-face and becoming captivated by the School of Athens, or the scientific point of view, for fourteen more years. That sums up my life, right up to the point where I discovered JP's conception of Christ and the final stage of my journey, the final mile of my ascent began. This final stage consists of another change in perspective but this one requires adopting a point of view that isn't physically possible within the Room of the Signatura. This is because the final perspective unites both of these frescoes. This point of view becomes possible only by getting my story straight, as it were. And, in my case, this means aligning and looking through all three layers of the composite lens at once.

Before being exposed to JP's ideas, my story, it seemed to me, consisted of three different and distinct stories rather than a single narrative. Because of the nihilistic attitude that came with the scientific point of view, I didn't even believe that I might have a purpose and that my story might actually constitute anything resembling a single coherent narrative. But JP challenged me to get my story straight and that meant looking for the thread that tied everything together. When I started thinking along those lines, I found myself trying to align all three chapters. Ignoring the middle layer for now, this idea can be represented by imagining looking at The Dispute through the School of Athens. While this point of view isn't possible within the Stanza, it is possible when I look back at my life. Doing this brings these two opposing points of view into alignment with each other. This final view, the one that looks through all three layers of the composite lens, unites these two perspectives that have been placed at odds with each other.

We've been relying entirely on narrative, up to this point, to describe the three chapters of my life and the dominant worldview in each. Our intention has been to make the reordering of my internal structure visible. Now that we've drawn a verbal sketch of all three layers and detailed the way that they fit together, we're going to leverage images, or pictures to help us tell the story, a story that starts with The Dispute.

Image 2: The Disputation of the Holy Sacrament[10]

10   Raphael, Public domain, via Wikimedia Commons

File URL: https://upload.wikimedia.org/wikipedia/commons/6/61/Disputa_del_Sacramento_%28Rafael%29.jpg

The Dispute represents a worldview in which God is the central or foundational axiom. And, as we've seen, this fresco represents revealed truth. This fresco, however, represents a decidedly Catholic perspective, and for that reason, it is representative only of the first chapter in my life. The Dispute falls short of being able to accurately represent the second chapter in my life, even despite the fact that the central axiom in the second chapter is the same.

During the second chapter in my life I was a Protestant. This means I rejected all imagistic representations of **God** in accordance with the second commandment. JP, in *Beyond Order*, captures the essence of my perspective at that time. The second commandment, Thou shalt not make unto thee any graven image (Exodus 20:4), JP tells us, speaks to *the danger of worshipping false idols (by confusing the representation, or the image, with the ineffable it is supposed to represent).* Protestants take this very seriously, and I did too. So, if we are going to represent the second chapter of my life imagistically, we need something that doesn't violate the second commandment and yet captures the essence of this chapter. Fortunately, JP provides the ideal image for this particular purpose in one of his lectures on the Book of Genesis.

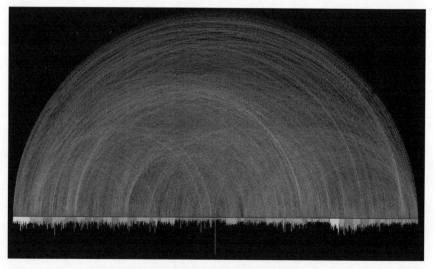

Image 3: Visualization (Bible cross-reference) [11]

---

11   Image by permission: Chris Harrison, Carnegie Mellon University, USA.

I've already mentioned the centrality of the Bible during the second chapter of my life and how I'd developed and maintained the practice of reading the Bible daily. This daily reading was only the beginning. I didn't just read the Bible; I studied it, meditated on it, and did my best to put it into practice in every aspect of my life. It's just fitting, then, that this chapter of my life be represented imagistically with a visualization of the Bible. That's what the above image represents. More specifically, this image shows the network of cross-references within the Bible.[12] Through countless hours of reading and studying, I internalized this visualization and used it to "paint over" the images from the first chapter of my life. In this way, by the end of the second chapter in my life, the Protestant view all but completely covered up the images of my youth.

This paints a pretty good picture my internal structure by the end of the second chapter. To be truly accurate, however, we need to preserve a minimum of information from the bottom layer. We can think of this as the most significant elements of The Dispute "bleeding through," as it were. As we've already mentioned, God, the central axiom of the religious point of view, spans both the first and second chapters. This means we need to bring the most essential elements represented in The Dispute to the foreground but in such a manner that the actual image is left behind. The following imaged does just that.

---

12   https://www.chrisharrison.net/index.php/Visualizations/BibleViz

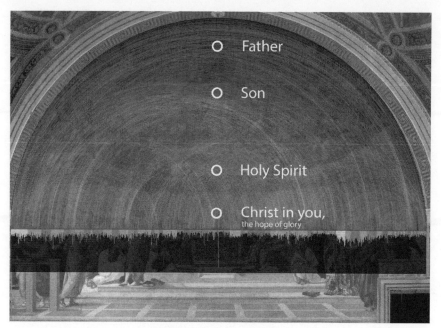

Image 4: Layers 1 and 2

As you can see, we've preserved the four essential features from Raphael's Dispute and carried them forward. Those elements include the godhead, God represented in the three persons of the Trinity: Father, Son, and Holy Spirit. The fourth element, the central theme of The Dispute, the Holy Sacrament or the Eucharist is also brought to the foreground. Together these elements represent God and the *incarnation of the Logos*. As you can see, all of these elements are represented verbally, using "the word" rather than an image to represent the idea. The only other thing worth noting here is that I've chosen the words *"Christ in you, the hope of glory"* from Colossians 1:27 to represent what the Eucharist represents, rather literally, to the Catholic.

That brings us to the transition from the second to the third chapter of my life. The third chapter starts with me walking away from God which can be illustrated as a turning from The Dispute to face Raphael's School of Athens.

Image 5: The School of Athens[13]

The School of Athens, as we've seen, represents natural truth or the scientific mode of construing the world. It does so by depicting the great thinkers of antiquity, like Plato and Aristotle, to represent their ideas. Of course, since it was painted in the early 1500s it fails to capture the development in our understanding of natural truth that has taken place since then. For this reason, we need to modify this image a bit in order to bring it up to date. More specifically, we want to ensure that we represent the three revolutions in the physical sciences that occurred in the twentieth century, our Trinity of Physics as it were. This update wouldn't be complete, however, if we didn't also integrate JP's conception of Christ. Keeping in mind that JP is a scientist, his conception of Christ can rightly be considered an advancement within the domain of natural truth, and so its proper place is in the School of Athens and not in The Dispute. This means, of course, that we require an imagistic representation of JP's conception of Christ.

---

13   By Raphael - Stitched together from vatican.va, Public Domain, https://commons.
      wikimedia.org/w/index.php?curid=4406048

Image 6: JP's Christ - Symbolically represented

This image contains all the essential elements of JP's conception of Christ in symbolic form. Working our way from the outside, we see the Uroboros, which reminds us of the fact that JP's conception of Christ is a process, an iterative process. The fact that the Uroboros is eating its tail reminds us that this process is a feedback loop. The diamond, which is "set" in the serpent's head, represents the conscious aspect of this process, the part that discriminates between "in the set" and "outside the set," which corresponds to The Responsibility Process. To indicate this we've etched the initials TRP into the diamond. We've also etched the number six into each of the lower or bottom facets of the diamond. The lower half of the diamond has been drawn to resemble carbon that has not yet been transformed into diamond. Together these elements represent the six Coping mindsets that we must repeatedly reject.

When taken as a whole, this image reminds us of God's words to the serpent in the garden. Foreshadowing Christ's victory over Satan. God says to the Serpent, "He will crush your head, and you will strike his heel" (Genesis 3:15). Finally, the Mandelbrot set sits at the center as a visual reminder of the process that mediates between order and chaos which helps us remain clear about Responsibility and Coping.

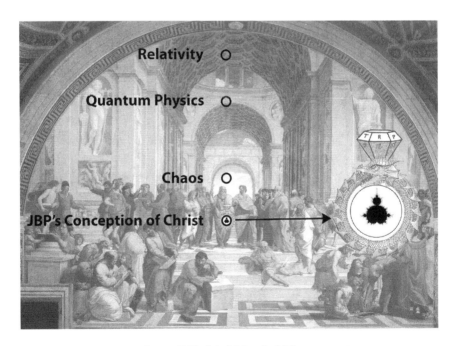

Image 7: Updated School of Athens

This modified School of Athens is now up to date. As you can see, we've been strategic about how to incorporate the new elements, the revolutions in the physical sciences, and JP's conception of Christ. As you can see, we've updated the School of Athens in such a way that it not only includes our additional developments in natural truth but does so in such a way as to allow us to connect it to The Dispute. That is, we've placed Relativity, Quantum Physics, and Chaos, our *Trinity of Physics* or *Trinity of Natural Truth,* onto the canvas in such a way that they align with the positions of the Father, Son, and Holy Spirit, the Trinity of Revealed Truth in The Dispute. Also, we've positioned JP's conception of Christ so that it corresponds to the position of the Eucharist in The Dispute. The placement of these elements was chosen to help us see how Natural Truth and Revealed Truth relate.

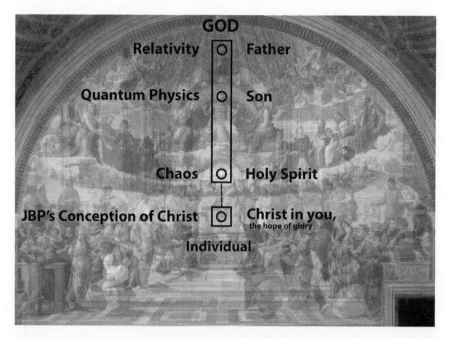

Image 8: Layers 1 and 3 Combined

While rather messy visually, this final image clearly illustrates how the layers fit together.[14] It's worth noting that there are two separate threads holding these layers together. The first is the embodiment of Christ and the second is God. The embodiment of Christ speaks to a connection at the level of human experience. This thread weaves through the Catholic Eucharist, the Protestant idea of Christ *in us* as our *hope of glory*, and JP's conception of Christ. Embodiment is the key. For a Catholic, the Eucharist represents the literal body of Christ. During every mass, it is believed that the Eucharist is transformed into the flesh of Christ by the priest and then, during the sacrament of communion, the individual believer takes that, puts it in his mouth, and eats it. This ceremony, then, is meant to be the literal eating or internalizing of Christ. Protestants reject the idea that the Eucharist literally becomes the body of Christ but this doesn't mean that they reject the idea of embodying Christ. That's why we used Colossians 1:27 to make this point. Finally, we've spent enough time considering JP's ideas to see how embodying Christ is central to his conception of Christ. And thanks to CA's TRP we know that this process, this little-known process in our minds, is already embodied as well as how it serves to mediate between order and chaos.

I've spoken of my first encounter with The Responsibility Process as corresponding to this event that is the discovering *my dead father*. Technically, that's incorrect. What I found inside the beast was Christ, *this process*. It was by embodying this process that I came to rediscover my dead Father—God. Consistent with the Biblical idea that we only know God through Christ, TRP and JP's conception of Christ led me back to the surface. It was only at that point that I recognized my dead Father in the Trinity of Physics. With that, a new conception of God was born within me. For all practical purposes, however, I did discover my dead father in that beast. Only it would take years and the discovery of JP's conception of Christ to bring it to the very surface of conscious awareness.

---

14   We've left the second layer out for clarity's sake. Just think of it as being transparent since the Bible is "The precondition for the manifestation of the Truth," and our focus is on the two representations of Truth.

God is that which eternally dies and is reborn in the pursuit of being and truth. https://youtu.be/h1oaSt60b0o?t=5277

What the final image represents, then, is the reconciliation of natural and revealed truth. That is my current lens of perception, these three layers all working together to make sense of reality from both modes of construing the world at once. The lens was constructed over a period of just under sixty years in three separate and distinct stages, the three chapters of my life. Each chapter is set within a particular worldview and, in order to move from one chapter to the next required taking out one lens and replacing it with another, required abandoning one system of belief and adopting a new one. This is the letting of my *old beliefs burn away* as part of the death and rebirth process. The first of these cycles of death and rebirth, the movement from the Catholic view to the Protestant view, lasted only a couple of years since both share the same foundation. The second iteration of this cycle of death and rebirth, the movement from the religious mode of construing the world to the scientific, was much more grueling. It required an eight-year descent into the nihilistic void followed by a decade-long ascent to the surface with my dead father. And even as I write these words, I'm reminded that the ascent isn't over till I've transmitted what I've learned through all of this.

Who could you be?

In *Beyond Order*, JP tells us: *When you face a challenge, you grapple with the world and inform yourself. This makes you more than you are. It makes you increasingly into who you could be. Who could you be? You could be all that a man or woman might be. You could be the newest avatar, in your own unique manner, of the great ancestral heroes of the past. This raises the question,* "What exactly would the newest avatar of my great ancestral heroes of the past look like?" Perhaps this question might be better framed this way: "What might the newest avatar of the great ancestral heroes of the Western mythological drama look like?"

This mythic life is symbolically represented by the savior—the individual who embodies the essential aspects of the mythological drama. In the Western tradition, for better or worse, like it or not—that individual is Christ.

– Maps of Meaning

Perhaps the newest avatar in this lineage might be the first to see Christ at His "appearing" or "revelation." I know that if I could be the newest avatar, in my own unique way, of the great ancestral heroes of my past, that's precisely who I would be.

But that's insane!

4.
WEAVING TOGETHER

Insane?

If you're having experiences that are beyond the norm, unless you can incorporate them back into your culture, you're alienated from your culture and that's a terrifying thing. It means you might be the only person that's insane like you. And you know it's very intolerable for people. It's bad enough to be different but to be so different that you're incomprehensible, to me that's the sort of horror you don't want to encounter.

So, the shaman are people who are possessed by a rich inner fantasy life but who are simultaneously capable of taking that and weaving it into the mythology that they are part of. That's what makes them sane rather than insane. https://youtu.be/k_yiezLqdVU?t=343

You might say that I too am *possessed of a rich inner fantasy life?* Within this fantasy, I imagine all sorts of connections between JP's conception of Christ and JG's process that reveals the Mandelbrot set and further connections to CA's TRP. Everything within this fantasy seems to make sense. All the dots fit together beautifully. But these dots suggest that I have been cast to play the role of the cultural revolutionary hero, the first person to recognize Christ's *return.* Believing this, however, suggests I might merely be insane. Fortunately, JP offers a way of testing whether I'm sane or have merely gotten lost within this *experience that is beyond the norm,* this fantasy, which, at this point has become my reality. The *sanity test* that JP puts forward seems rather strange, to tell the truth. The idea that my sanity or insanity can be determined by my ability to weave my experience back into the culture of which I am a part seems like a rather odd test. Nevertheless, if that is the test, then it is time to see if I can in fact weave my experience into my culture's central myth, the Judeo-Christian myth.

It seems to me that we've already encountered this idea of weaving an experience back into the culture's mythology. This idea seems equivalent to the idea of the revolutionary hero *furthering* his culture's central myth: *The revolutionary hero opens himself up to the possibility of advancement—to furtherance of his culture's central myth* (MoM). This, it would seem, is what constitutes a return to community, since *the second stage of the hero's journey is return to the community (MoM).* And so, the question that this chapter seeks to resolve is whether or not I am sane. As insane as it might sound, if I am actually sane, this means that my purpose has been to play the role of the cultural revolutionary hero.

The story of two books

I've watched the "debates" between JP and Sam Harris (SH) a couple of times now. The first time, I hadn't yet read anything that either man had written. The second time, however, I was very familiar with each man's thinking and this allowed me to really enter into the issues they were discussing. If you watch these talks, you'll notice that they keep coming back to one issue in particular. The issue that they seem to be most at odds over reminds me of something from my fundamentalist past:

> *God wrote two books—the Christian theologians say—the book of nature and the book of Scripture. The first is common revelation because everyone has this book and everyone can read it—"Day to day pours forth speech, and night to night declares knowledge" (Psalms 19:2). The second book is special revelation because this is given in a book to the literate minority of mankind... The first book*

is called natural revelation because it is derived from nature and human nature: "For the invisible things of him from the creation of the world are clearly seen, being understood by the things that are made, even his eternal power and Godhead" (Rom. 1:20).

The second book is called supernatural revelation for though it contains and confirms truths revealed by nature, it also contains what is above and beyond nature, though never, strictly speaking, contrary to it. If the first book is produced by divine creation, the second is by divine inspiration. "All scripture is given by inspiration of God, and is profitable for doctrine, for reproof, for correction, for instruction in righteousness" (2 Tim. 3:16; cf. Ps. 19:7 ff).

– John H. Gerstner, *The Rational Biblical Theology of Jonathan Edwards*

If this sounds familiar, it should. The idea being expressed here is essentially the same idea represented in Raphael's The Dispute on the Blessed Sacrament and the School of Athens. As we saw in the previous chapter, the former represents revealed truth, which is equivalent to the book of *supernatural revelation;* while the latter, the book of *common revelation,* corresponds to natural truth. This idea that God wrote two books or that there are two separate and distinct wellsprings of truth lies at the heart of the debates between JP and SH.

Both these men, as scientists, implicitly acknowledge the authority of the book of Nature. They find common ground there. The tension or conflict between the two arises specifically from JP's willingness to speak of the Bible in such a way as to acknowledge that it constitutes another source of Truth. JP never comes out and says that God wrote two books, but SH recognizes that JP treats the Bible as if it were a separate source of truth, as if it were true, and that's an accurate assessment:

Mythological renditions of history, like those in the Bible, are just as "true" as the standard Western empirical renditions, just as literally true, but how they are true is different. Western historians describe (or think they describe) "what" happened. The traditions of mythology and religion describe the significance of what happened (and it must be noted that if what happens is without significance, it is irrelevant).

– Maps of Meaning

Throughout the debates, SH keeps coming back to this one issue. He seems hell-bent on getting JP to treat the Bible as just another book. We don't even need to listen very carefully to observe that SH seems to hold the position that it is a scientist's obligation to be closed-minded about Scripture, and that it is every scientist's duty to place the Bible on the same shelf as all other works of fiction, the category he assigns the Bible to. So, it's not as if SH's observations about JP's attitude toward the Bible are wrong. JP may not fully agree with the theologians, but he definitely demonstrates something resembling the theologian's position.

Personally, I find it ironic to observe just how closed-minded SH is about the Bible, considering that one of his biggest complaints about fundamentalists is that they are closed-minded. The *theologically sound* Christian, however, is not at liberty to be closed-minded with respect to what is revealed in the book of Nature. Many, if not most, Bible believers are not theologically sound, however. And wherever you hear someone assert that God only wrote one book they are demonstrating just that. While SH wouldn't word it this way, what he is essentially saying is that God wrote only one book, the book of Nature. In this way, SH is making the same mistake as the person who claims God only wrote one book, the Bible. Each forgets that God wrote two books, and uses their preferred source of truth as license to deny or dismiss the authority of the other book authored by God. This is precisely the same as adopting one of the two valid ways of construing the world and setting it at odds with the other, ignoring the fact that both are needed for a complete world-picture. JP, however, seems to recognize that throwing away one of these books, one of these modes of construing the world, is equivalent to plucking out one of your eyes. You may be able to see things as clearly as before but you've thrown away your depth perception.

Those who, like SH or his "Christian" counterparts, those who insist that God wrote only one book, are taking the easy way out. Just set the two at odds, pick a side, and insist the other side has it wrong. No need to contend with reconciling the two. Just invalidate one of God's books using what is revealed in the other, and—poof—problem solved. In MoM, JP expresses what is essentially SH's position this way: *The great forces of empiricism and rationality and the great technique of the experiment have killed myth, and it cannot be resurrected.* The sentence, however, doesn't end there and it's the end of the sentence that punctuates the difference between the way these two men think about the Bible. By leaving the ending off, the sentence expresses SH's position precisely. To accurately reflect JP's thinking, however, we need the entire sentence: *The great forces of empiricism and rationality and the great technique of the experiment have killed myth, and it cannot be resurrected—or so it seems.* With those last four words, JP opens up a can of worms that SH would prefer to keep sealed tight. Ironically enough, it's fundamentalist *dogma* that prevented me from using this trick of invalidating one of God's books using the other. It was *sound doctrine* that prevented me from being closed-minded about the book of Nature. I simply wasn't allowed to short circuit the process in this way. Instead, I had no option but to wrestle with both books even though I did have to defer to the Bible in all matters pertaining to salvation, a subject the book of Nature is silent on anyway.

The question that immediately arises is how do you deal with the apparent contradictions between these two books? If you're going to entertain the possibility that God may have written two books, then you're going to need a way to face the contradictions. The approach I used was to follow Mary's example. Scripture provides us with a window into how Jesus' mother Mary dealt with the things she couldn't understand, allowing us to see how she dealt with the *anomalies* she encountered. Consider, for instance, the story in Luke's Gospel about the 12-year-old Jesus remaining behind after the feast of Passover and how his parents eventually found him in the temple. We can see that Mary is thrown off balance by the interaction with her son. We can tell she can't quite make sense of the interaction. So what does she do? Does she just shrug it off with a "Well, that's Jesus for you?" She does not. Instead, we read that Mary, "his mother kept all these sayings in her heart." Mary doesn't ignore the strange things she encounters but keeps them or gathers them in her heart where they won't be forgotten. This is the example I followed. Like Mary, I chose not to hide from these sorts of things but to face them, do my best to resolve them, and, failing that, gather them together in a folder labeled "unresolved—not yet integrated."

From paradigm to paradigm

There's an idea that JP takes a lot of time developing in MoM, that's extremely relevant to this discussion. That idea is that the known has a paradigmatic structure. What makes this idea so significant is the implications that it has on the way that we learn new things. Learning involves *exploratory activity,* and this activity generally results in our *known* being modified. This modification may involve *restriction, expansion, or transformation* of this structure depending on what the exploration had to teach. But learning involves discovering error in our current understanding. If this exploration leads to the discovery of a *major error,* then *such activity culminates in "revolution": in modification of the entire story guiding affective evaluation and behavioral programming.* Saying this another way, a revolutionary transformation of the known is required whenever the foundation of the known, the axioms upon which the paradigm rests, are revealed to be false.

JP makes a connection between the paradigmatic structure of the known and our stories. Our stories are our description of the known. And so, an update to the paradigmatic structure of the known takes the form of an update to our stories. That is, modifications to our *life-story* are equivalent to modifications of our *known.* These don't have to be major modifications. As JP makes clear, they can occur at any scale. "Small scale irritations require minor life-story modifications. Large-scale catastrophes, by contrast, undermine everything." The "biggest disasters" occur when the largest stories that we play out are threatened with dissolution, as a consequence of radical "environmental" transformation. The *largest stories that we play out* is an obvious reference to the culture's central myth. And we've already seen how our social environment has been transformed by *the great forces of empiricism and rationality and the great technique of the experiment,* which have *killed myth*. Alluding to the Judeo-Christian myth, JP sums this up this way: "If the presuppositions of a theory have been invalidated, argues Nietzsche, then the theory has been invalidated."

Considering all these ideas together, what we find is that the West is currently in the midst of a disaster at the largest possible scale, a disaster that has resulted in the dissolution of the most fundamental stories that we play out. Following this thinking through to its natural conclusion, the West is facing an existential crisis that requires an update to or complete rewriting of its central stories. Understanding this allows us to see our current place in history. Our culture's central myth has been *killed*, has fallen into dissolution, and we haven't yet updated that story. That means that the West currently finds itself without a grand narrative, living in the void between narratives. And since narrative is the force that unites a culture, this implies that the fabric of the culture is currently going through a *period of dissolution*. Left unresolved, this catastrophe will play itself out, *naturally,* through the continued and, eventually, final dissolution of the culture itself through the loss of its key beliefs.

Earlier we touched on the idea of storing up anomalies. This idea is extremely significant within the context of moving from one paradigm to another. Successfully moving from one paradigm to another depends, to a large extent, on a couple of key elements. First, success depends on having a clear enough picture of the current paradigm. A blurry conception of the current state will not suffice. Next, we need enough anomalies to convince ourselves that the current paradigm is insufficient. This insufficiency is what motivates us to allow the current paradigm to dissolve which is essentially the same as diving into the void. But we don't want to act too quickly. Acting prematurely, abandoning the existing paradigm before we've gathered enough information can leave us stuck in limbo, having walked away from the old but unable to construct a new paradigm. Strike out too soon and the void will swallow you whole, and you'll never find your way back to the surface. That's where the West finds itself today. That's the problem that JP and SH are contending with and the reason JP keeps bringing it up:

> *There's an ancient idea, a very ancient idea, that when you face the void, what you do is confront it and leap into it. And what you discover at the bottom is a beast and inside that beast you discover your dead father, lying dead, and then you re-animate your father and you bring him back to the surface and that's the means of dealing with the void.* https://youtu.be/aALsFhZKg-Q?t=6135

> *We have to go back into the past and find the wisdom that can help guide us because we don't have to do this as if we're encountering everything for the first time. And that's exactly the idea of going into the void to rescue your father. And that is the eternal age-old medication for the confrontation of the void.* https://youtu.be/aALsFhZKg-Q?t=6319

The clock is ticking

Reality is dynamic and not static. The effects of the dissolution of the myth continue to play out in society. This means that the fabric of society will continue to dissolve until the problem is rectified or the culture collapses entirely. This explains the sense of urgency with which JP presses SH when he concludes: "Do we have to go into the past, to rescue what's best, given the understanding that there is something there worth rescuing or not?!" In fact the sense of urgency is so great that the discussion takes a sidestep at one point to discuss the idea of slowing down the disintegration of the culture. You can see this clearly expressed here:

> *One of the things Douglas [Murray] has pointed out was that there are things that we've done in free countries, let's say broadly speaking in the West that are worth protecting and that in order to protect them in the longest sense, it's conceivable that we need a, a cognitive structure, something like that that can act as a bulwark against those forces that would seek to undermine and destroy it. And Douglas has been driven, I would say, to some degree, to hypothesize that Christianity, for all its faults, or we could say Judeo-Christianity to broaden it, for all its faults might provide something approximating that bulwark if we could only figure out how to utilize it properly.* https://youtu.bs://youtu.be/PqpYxD71hJU?t=1419

When an atheist suggests that we might need to turn to Judeo-Christianity in order to slow the cultural rate of decay, we have reason to pause and consider just how serious this decay really is. There is no going backward, of course. And that's why JP wants to go back to the past "to rescue what's best." But here JP reveals a chink in his mental armor. First he forgets that he already knows what needs to be "rescued" and that is *That which was the holiest and mightiest of all that the world has yet possessed.* Just as importantly, though, JP seems to forget that *going back to the past* is not an academic exercise. More precisely, the type of knowledge of the past that's required in order to successfully move from one paradigm to another is of the "knowledge of" variety and not merely "knowledge about." The knowledge of the past must be internalized experiential knowledge of the past and this type of knowledge can only be acquired through apprenticeship. Knowing about the past isn't good enough, because that sort of knowledge isn't *embodied* and therefore cannot really be said to have taken shape within the individual. Without proper *enculturation* the individual lacks the vital, implicit information, the information that hasn't yet been rendered explicit and which comes only from embodying the story. This is critical, because the hero, an individual, is *the first to have his internal structure reorganized.* Without proper enculturation this structure never forms. Knowledge *about* is no substitute for knowledge *of*, which is the true prerequisite to a successful descent into, and, most importantly, a successful ascent out of, the void. By inviting SH to *go back into the past* or to *leap into* the void, JP is demonstrating an insufficient understanding of what he himself has spelled out.

Back to apprenticeship

> *...two things are happening at once, during an apprenticeship worthy of the name (just as learning to play a game and learning to be a good sport happen at the same time, while playing). Initially, the apprentice must become a servant of tradition, of structure, and of dogma, just as the child who wants to play must follow the rules of the game. At its best, this servitude means grateful alliance, in one form or another, with the institutions typically considered patriarchal. Apprenticeship means heat and pressure (as new workmen are tried by their peers, as articling law students are tried by their employers, as medical residents are tried by physicians, nurses, and patients). The goal of this heat and pressure is subordination of an undeveloped personality (by no means "individual" at this point) to a single path, for the purposes of transformation from undisciplined beginner to accomplished master.*

> *The master, who is the rightful product of apprenticeship, is, however, no longer the servant of dogma. Instead, he is now himself served by dogma, which he has the responsibility to maintain as well as the right to change, when change is necessary. This makes the master, who once allowed himself to be enslaved, an emergent follower of spirit—the wind (spirit) that bloweth where it listeth (John 3:8). The master can allow himself his intuitions, as the knowledge obtained by the discipline he has acquired will enable him to criticize his own ideas and assess their true value. He may therefore more clearly perceive the fundamental patterns*

or principles that underlie the dogmas of his discipline, and draw inspiration from those, instead of blindly adhering to the rules as currently articulated or embodied. He may even rely on the integrated union of his personality and his training to modify or transform even those more fundamental, deeply intuited principles, in the service of an even higher union.

– Beyond Order

There are a few points about this apprenticeship process worth highlighting. First, it's critical to note that apprenticeship is domain specific. The process of apprenticeship takes an *undisciplined beginner* and transforms them into an *accomplished master* within a particular domain. The apprenticeship of a medical resident doesn't produce a master within the domain of law. In the same way, apprenticeship in a scientific domain like psychology, let's say, doesn't produce a master within the domain of religion. Here's where a lot of confusion arises with respect to JP, because he appears to have done just that. He seems to have apprenticed in psychology and become a master in Christianity. But the master must have served dogma and not simply be informed about it. And, from what I can see, there is simply no evidence that JP has ever served Christian dogma. His *discipline* may have a lot in common with Christianity, but Christianity and psychology are two distinct domains. Having never served Judeo-Christian dogma, by JP's own reasoning, it is impossible for him to have become a master in that domain. I, on the other hand, can honestly say that I have served Judeo-Christian dogma, and that over an extended period of time. And so, I can lay claim to being the rightful product of apprenticeship within this particular domain.

The master is the rightful product of apprenticeship. This implies that this apprenticeship process is the only valid path to mastery. And mastery is of critical importance because only the master *has the responsibility to maintain* but more importantly for our purpose, *the right to change* that *dogma which he once served but now is served by.* Only the master can update the story! It's the master, after all, who is most likely to ...*more clearly perceive the fundamental patterns or principles that underlie the dogmas of his discipline.* It appears, then, that since I consider myself the genuine product of this apprenticeship process under Christ, that it is my responsibility both to maintain this dogma and my right to update it, when required.

Given that it's my responsibility to maintain the dogma of my discipline, we're going to turn our attention to what JP gets wrong concerning the Bible. His mistake lies in his approach to the Bible. JP looks at the Bible through the lens of psychology. The problem with this approach is that it fails to enter into the Biblical narrative deeply enough. There is only one lens through which the Bible can be correctly perceived, and that is the Bible itself. What I mean by that is that the Bible is a self-referential system and it's for this reason that the Bible can only correctly be interpreted in its own light. JP knows this. He even quotes Nietzsche as saying that *Christianity is a system, a consistently thought out and complete view of things.* Using an external frame of reference through which to interpret the Bible guarantees you're going to misinterpret it, that you're going to miss the mark.

The Bible's Protagonist

Here's a simple question for you. Imagine I had read a book, a book that was rumored to tell the most glorious story. Now imagine you asked me to tell you about this story and I do just that. Only, as I'm retelling the story I decide I'm going to "cancel" the protagonist. That is, I give an account of the story, but I don't say anything about the main character, nothing about his actions or the consequences of his actions, nothing about the intentions and motivations underlying his actions, nothing at all. I essentially erase the protagonist from the story altogether. The question is this: "How faithful to the original story do you think this rendition can possibly be?" It should be obvious that whatever the retold version of the story turns out to be, no matter how faithful it is to the remaining details, it will not be the same story, not even close. Any story in which the protagonist is entirely removed becomes, of necessity, an entirely different story. This is precisely what JP does when he lectures on the Bible, but he does it so subtly that it's barely noticeable, at least to the untrained ear.

For better or worse, like it or not, the Protagonist in the Bible is God, our dead Father. When JP lectures on the Bible from the psychological perspective he is circumventing, which is to say, entirely ignoring the true Protagonist. In fact, in taking this approach with the Bible, JP, whether consciously or unconsciously, goes one step further. Instead of simply removing the Protagonist, JP does something far worse: he tells the story substituting the antagonist for the Protagonist. Listen carefully to JP and you'll see that he's telling a story in which man is the protagonist. This psychological approach places man at the center, allowing JP to dismiss God and God's role in the story. JP still gets very close to the story because he still deals with the effects of the true Protagonist's actions but without actually acknowledging Him.

This fundamental pattern of making man the protagonist is also evident in MoM. Consider, for example, that despite using the word "God" over five-hundred times, MoM is literally godless. Faith is present everywhere in MoM, but the object of that faith, with only one exception and that only when quoting someone else, is never God. JP talks of *faith in personal ability, faith in the conditions of experience, faith in human potential* which he equates with *the individual spirit, faith in the heroic, faith in oneself, faith in the ideal, faith in our central natures, faith in the future, faith in the human essence,* and even *faithful adherence to the reality of personal experience*—but never faith in God. This is significant.

The Apostle Paul, writing to Timothy and speaking of the last days, warns of men who "have a form of godliness" but who "deny the power thereof" (2 Timothy 3:5). I'm pointing directly at JP here because he has ventured into my domain, a domain in which I bear a responsibility to *maintain dogma.* Watch the debates between SH and JP and what you'll see is that all four of the men who played a part in these debates are exemplars of the type of *behavior* that Paul is targeting. All four of these men, JP, SH, and the two moderators, Bret Weinstein and Douglas Murray, are certainly *moral* individuals, individuals who clearly *have a form of godliness* but all of them, JP included, are operating from the perspective that *God is dead* and thus they deny God. What's especially interesting about these four and this particular set of debates is that their intention comes across very clearly. They recognize the impending collapse of Western culture and are desperately looking for a way to prevent this from happening. What is equally obvious is that they have no idea how to do that.

But getting back to JP and his approach to the Bible, we might ask how he can possibly understand the Bible if he substitutes the antagonist, man, for the Protagonist, God? The answer is that he can't. Sure, he can gain a lot of insights from the text using his approach, but what good are these insights if they blind him from seeing the most significant elements of the narrative? Recall that successfully moving from one paradigm to the next requires a solid, accurate grasp of the current paradigm. Our intention in pointing out JP's errors, therefore, is not to disparage JP but to ensure that we are clear about the starting point, the original paradigm, in this case, the Biblical narrative, as a whole.

The master has a responsibility to maintain dogma because we don't want to throw out the baby with the bath water but also because the way forward depends on a correct understanding of the past. And, in this context, the past is the myth itself. On the plus side, having an accurate understanding of the current paradigm increases the likelihood that the way forward will reveal itself. It's critically important to recognize that movement forward consists of movement from one paradigm to another, and that this doesn't necessarily require making any changes to the story itself. That is, updating our understanding of the story, without changing the story, also constitutes movement from one paradigm to another. The reason this is so critical is that the story in question, the Bible, ends with a rather severe warning not to alter the story:

18 I warn everyone who hears the words of the prophecy of this scroll: If anyone adds anything to them, God will add to that person the plagues described in this scroll. 19 And if anyone takes words away from this scroll of prophecy, God will take away from that person any share in the tree of life and in the Holy City, which are described in this scroll.

– Revelation 22:18-19

In removing the Protagonist from His own story, JP has no way of understanding the Bible as a whole. It's only through its Protagonist that the most fundamental patterns and key dogmas of the Biblical narrative can be understood. We therefore need a solid understanding of the Bible's narrative arc if we are to succeed in furthering the myth. We need to gather up all the most important dogmas, and reanimate the Protagonist in order to do that. What's critical here isn't dogma for dogma's sake but an understanding of the narrative *through* dogma. There's a difference between believing the story and believing what the story teaches. We're interested in what it teaches in order to get the story straight, from a within-the-narrative perspective, so regardless of our feelings or opinions about the dogma, we're going to accept it at face value in order to understand the narrative as a whole.

What's the Bible about? Part 1

What is the Bible about? The shortest answer is that the Bible tells the story of a promise, a promise made in eternity (Revelation 13:8), and the unfolding of that promise in time (Titus 1:1-3), in human history. This promise constitutes an arrangement, or agreement, within the Godhead, which is to say an agreement between the Father, Son, and Holy Ghost with each "Person" of the Trinity agreeing to enact their own particular part of this agreement. This "covenant" is necessitated by an inevitable problem that would invariably arise as a result of the act of creation. God, foreseeing this unavoidable problem, "the fall of man," takes it upon Himself to resolve it. So the Bible tells the story of how God has taken Responsibility for this problem and devised a solution, as well as the effective means of bringing that solution into being. The Bible tells this story, which starts in eternity past, from before the beginning of time and then, starting with creation it reveals the unfolding of that plan in time, to the very end, when the solution becomes fully manifested and the problem finally and permanently resolved.

The Bible, then, is a story about God's intention, His commitment to resolve the problem of the *fall* and to restore mankind to his original state. With that, let's turn our attention to the fall. We'll start by assuming that JP is correct about the nature of the *fall of man,* which is the emergence of consciousness or perhaps more accurately, self-consciousness. Let's also assume that he is correct with respect to the *two transpersonal patterns of behavior* that emerge as a result of the *contamination of anomaly with the threat of death,* and that these two patterns represent the two possible attitudes toward *confrontation with the unknown.* All of these ideas are consistent with Scripture, though in the Bible, the ideas are expressed in mythological language. Here's how the Bible articulates the same ideas:

> *14 Inasmuch then as the children have partaken of flesh and blood, He Himself likewise shared in the same, that through death He might destroy him who had the power of death, that is, the devil, 15 and release those who through fear of death were all their lifetime subject to bondage.*
>
> – Hebrews 2:14-15

Notice how "fear of death," perhaps the ultimate unknown, enslaves us to the adversarial tendency, the devil. Notice, also, the role that fear plays in this captivity. This is embodiment of the adversarial tendency: *The other "son of God" is the eternal adversary. This "spirit of unbridled rationality," horrified by his limited apprehension of the conditions of existence, shrinks from contact with everything he does not understand. This shrinking weakens his personality, no longer nourished by the "water of life," and makes him rigid and authoritarian, as he clings desperately to the familiar, "rational," and stable. Every deceitful retreat increases his fear.* (MoM)

The language may be different but the ideas are the same. Consciousness, the awareness of our own mortality, and the *contamination of anomaly with the threat of death* all work together to drive us to turn from God and embody the adversarial spirit in which we allow ourselves to be dominated by fear. It's this turning away from God, this "separation from God," which constitutes the most significant aspect of the fall. And so, the *personality that is no longer nourished by the "water of life"* is the soul that is no longer in a life-sustaining relationship with God. This is the problem statement.

This is also where JP's thinking goes sideways, because he lacks sufficient understanding of Christian doctrine. One such doctrine is the doctrine of the *total depravity of man*, the idea that man is completely and utterly incapable of resolving the effect of *the fall*. That is, sound Biblical doctrine maintains that the fall is a problem that man cannot fix himself. This brings us back to the distinction between works and grace. We've talked about the fall in psychological terms, in terms of consciousness, but we haven't looked at it from the Biblical perspective, the one we're interested in here. What is it about the fall, for instance, that makes "salvation" necessary? To understand the answer we need to put the Protagonist back into the story. We need the Protagonist in order to understand the fall, because what the fall represents at the most fundamental level of analysis is a change in "standing" before God. This change in standing is primarily relational in nature. And the relationship in question is the relationship between God and his creation, man, or mankind. Strip the Protagonist from the story and you have no way of understanding this.

Look at how all of this is made clear in the first few chapters of the Bible. Once the work of creation is complete, it's declared good, and not just good, but *very good* (Genesis 1:31). Immediately after the fall we are told that Adam and Eve *heard the sound of the Lord God walking in the garden in the cool of the day.* This gives us a glimpse into the intimate relationship that existed between God and his creation before the fall. We can only assume that before the fall, God "walked" very closely with His Creation. Then we are told that immediately after the eating of the forbidden fruit, upon hearing

God in the garden, Adam and Eve hide from God (Genesis 3:8). This hiding from God captures the essence of the true nature of the fall. What it reveals is that the original inner disposition of Adam and Eve towards God has changed. They are no longer in "right-standing" with God, and they know it. Where once they had been attracted to God, looking forward to walking and talking with God, now they're afraid and so they run away and hide. The nature of the problem, then, consists of an inner change within man that constitutes the loss of right-standing before God and the awareness of this in the form of fear, fear of God. What's more, in the Bible, this fear of God is directly connected to the fear of death, because God had warned Adam and Eve concerning this tree saying *for in the day that thou eatest thereof thou shalt surely die (Genesis 2:17)*. This permanent alteration in the disposition of the heart toward the ultimate unknowns, death and God, is the problem that the fall represents.

Salvation, then, can only be properly understood in light of the fall. Salvation speaks to the restoration of right-standing before God. When put in these terms, the distinction between works and grace starts to make sense. Works, in the Bible, is equivalent to merit, and whatever is merited is earned or deserved. The central idea, the axiom that underpins works, is the idea that right-standing before God is something that is within man's power to rectify, the idea that we can fix this problem on our terms. The Bible, however, is clear that right-standing before God can only be gained on God's terms. The very notion that we can act in such a way as to earn God's favor reveals just how wrong our thinking about God is. To earn something from someone is to put the other person under obligation. If we earn something, it is owed us. Works is a twisted mindset, a way of thinking, a childish way of thinking about God. To understand the doctrines of election and sovereign grace we must see them as serving to destroy all notions that we can somehow place God under obligation to accept us. Look at how Paul says precisely this: *Even so then at this present time also there is a remnant according to the election of grace. And if by grace, then is it no more of works:*

otherwise grace is no more grace. But if it be of works, then is it no more grace: otherwise work is no more work (Romans 11:5-6).

The question that immediately arises from this is, if salvation, or restored right-standing with God, cannot be earned, then how exactly is a person saved? The answer is profoundly simple. The Bible describes salvation in terms of a gift, a gift that can be freely accepted but can never be earned. *For by grace are ye saved through faith; and that not of yourselves: it is the gift of God* (Ephesians 2:8).

We've looked at paradigms and paradigm shifts enough at this point to be able to recognize that works and grace represent two mutually exclusive paradigms or mindsets. The fundamental axiom of the paradigm of works is "I can." I can earn my way into God's presence and favor. This axiom is anathema within the paradigm of grace, which recognizes that God cannot be placed under obligation or manipulated in any way. Grace recognizes God's holiness. The fundamental axiom of the paradigm is "I don't deserve" and "I can never deserve" or earn the "right" to be accepted in the presence of a holy God. But grace doesn't end there. Grace extends God's mercy to the individual by making right-standing with God something that is freely offered by God and everyone is free to accept this gift. That is the essence of Biblical faith. Faith accepts, it receives God's gift, as a gift. Faith receives freely what works can never attain.

Here we catch a glimpse of the necessity of the book of Scripture. Scripture reveals something that man can't find or derive from the book of Nature. The nature of the problem of the fall has to do with right-standing with God. The fall changed man's attitude toward death and the other ultimate form of the unknown, God. The fall represents this loss of right-standing with God. Salvation is the restoration of that right-standing, and this, is something that cannot be earned or merited in any way shape or form. To approach God from works, the mindset that thinks it either is or can become "good enough" to earn God's favor, is therefore not only ineffective but outright offensive to God. And it is only through Scripture that we can know this.

Satan pleads the law of works, but Christ pleads the law of grace.

– John Bunyan

The paradigmatic structure of works and grace reveals the difference in mindsets between these two ways of facing the Ultimate Unknown. These two mindsets are also, essentially, JP's "two transpersonal patterns of behavior and schemas of representation, comprising the individual as such, embodied in mythology as the 'hostile brothers.'" We should take careful note of what motivated the development of these two transpersonal patterns. "The 'contamination of anomaly with the threat of death,' attendant on the development of self-consciousness, amplifies the valence of the unknown to a virtually unbearable point. This unbearable amplification has motivated the development of two transpersonal patterns of behavior..." The salient point here, the one that JP misses because he has erased the Protagonist from the Bible, is that the fear of the threat of death is indistinguishable from the fear, the unhealthy fear, of God. This is also why removing the true Protagonist from the Biblical narrative completely changes the meaning of the story. All of the most critical fundamental patterns in the Bible are lost when the Protagonist is removed. Without its Protagonist, the Bible becomes nothing more than another self-help book meant to show us how to save ourselves by lifting Christ up as a mere example to be imitated, the very opposite of what the story teaches when the Protagonist remains central in the story.

To correctly understand the Biblical narrative and, by extension, the process that the New Testament is a description of, requires a correct understanding of the distinction between the two fundamental mindsets of works and grace. The latter is acceptable and pleasing to God while the former is offensive.

Fear of death = fear of God

This observation sets the stage for a fundamental realization: human beings do not learn to fear new objects or situations, or even really "learn" to fear something that previously appeared safe, when it manifests a dangerous property. Fear is the a priori position, the natural response to everything for which no structure of behavioral adaptation has been designed and inculcated.

– Maps of Meaning

We can correctly think of Scripture as articulating a *structure of behavioral adaptation* with respect to God. Get rid of the Bible and we are left without this structure, and the consequence is that God becomes something for which *no structure of behavioral adaptation has been designed and inculcated.* Under these conditions the default response, the *"natural"* response is fear, and in this case, specifically, fear of God, and, more accurately an unhealthy fear of God. This is the type of fear that motivates a flight response, a running away from God. What this means is that the natural response, the response of the "natural man" to God, is to hide, like Adam and Eve, and to run away like a point running off to infinity. The Bible expresses this idea this way: *The natural man does not accept the things that come from the Spirit of God* (1 Corinthians 2:14) and *As it is written, There is none righteous, no, not one: There is none that understandeth, there is none that seeketh after God"* (Romans 3:10-11). There is none that seeks after God! How can they seek after God when the natural response to God is fear, the kind of fear that runs away?

This *natural response* to God is tremendously significant because it sheds light on the true nature of the problem:

The world of order and chaos might be regarded as the stage, for man—for the twin aspects of man, more accurately: for the aspect that inquires, and explores (which voluntarily expands the domain and structure of order, culture) and for the aspect that opposes that inquiry, exploration and transformation. The great story is, therefore, good vs. evil, played out against the endless flux of being, as it signifies. The forces of "good" have an eternal character... unfortunately, so do the forces of evil.

This eternality exists because all members of the species Homo Sapiens are essentially equivalent, equal before God: we find our-selves vulnerable, mortal creatures, thrown into a universe bent on our creation and protection—and our transformation and destruction. Our "attitude" towards this ambivalent universe can only take one of two prototypical forms: positive or negative. The precise nature of these two forms (which can only be regarded as complex "personalities") —and of the background against which they work—constitutes the central subject matter of myth...

– Maps of Meaning

Take careful note that it's our **attitude towards** this ambivalent universe that is at the root of the problem of good and evil. If we put God back into the narrative, then it's but a small step to the realization that it's **our atti-tude toward God** that delineates between good and evil. This needs to be explored further.

Original sin and Coping

Let's return to TRP, and more specifically to the double line that delineates between Responsibility and Coping. Let's consider, for a moment, what JP tells us about the fundamental states of social being. *There are three funda-mental states of social being: tyranny (you do what want), slavery (I do what you want), or negotiation (Beyond Order).* These states of social being can easily be *mapped* to TRP. Negotiation obviously maps to Responsibility, which corresponds to the heroic tendency. Next, if we recognize the hostile brothers, the conjoined twins of tyranny and slavery as two sides of a single coin, we can see how these two states of social being map to Coping. These two fundamental states of social being, tyranny and slavery, are equivalent, therefore, to the adversarial tendency. Understanding the nature of Coping in this way allows us a window into the "soul" of the individual stuck in Coping mindsets.

We feel constrained and trapped, without options, when operating from Coping. What may not be immediately obvious is that when we embody Coping, we are operating from a position that is "internally split." The reason for this becomes apparent when we recognize that Coping represents abdication of Responsibility, represents refusal or inability to negotiate. What this means is that from within a Coping mindset, the only *states of social being* that are available are tyranny and slavery. This is true within the individual who has settled for Coping.

> ...archaic people found it easy to believe that the human soul was haunted by ghosts—possessed by ancestral spirits, demons, and gods—none of whom necessarily had the best interests of the person at heart. Since the time of the psychoanalysts, these contrary forces, these obsessive and sometimes malevolent spirits, have been conceptualized psychologically as impulses, emotions, or motivational states—or as complexes, which act like partial personalities united within the person by memory but not by intent. Our neurological structure is indeed hierarchical. The powerful instinctual servants at the bottom, governing thirst, hunger, rage, sadness, elation, and lust, can easily ascend and become our masters, and just as easily wage war with one another. The resilience and strength of a united spirit is not easy to attain.
>
> – Beyond Order

We can expand our understanding of the true nature of Responsibility and Coping by recognizing that they correspond to the ideas of a *united spirit* and a *divided spirit,* which is characterized by warring *partial personalities.*

We can also see that the warring *partial personalities* are enacting tyranny and slavery. The dominant partial personalities become *masters* or *tyrants* over the subordinate partial personalities that they enslave. We see, then, that within a single individual, one or more partial personalities may tyrannize and enslave the other partial personalities. Coping, then, represents a divided, split personality. And so, JP continues:

> *A house divided against itself, proverbially, cannot stand. Likewise,*
> *a poorly integrated person cannot hold himself together when*
> *challenged. He loses union at the highest level of psychological*
> *organization. He loses the properly balanced admixture of prop-*
> *erties that is another feature of the well-tempered soul, and cannot*
> *hold his self together. We know this when we say "He lost it" or*
> *"He just fell apart." Before he picks up the pieces and rearranges*
> *them, such a person is likely to fall prey to domination by one or*
> *more partial personalities.*
>
> – Beyond Order

Note how the person, the individual, falls prey and is dominated by the dominant partial personality. Lacking either the will or the requisite skills, the individual who is OK with Coping resides in a perpetual state of internal conflict. *Negotiation is exceptionally difficult,* JP tells us before pointing out that *there are the tricks that people use, too, to avoid negotiation.* This should call to mind the idea that TRP is *a little-known pattern in our minds that determines how we process thoughts about taking and avoiding responsibility.* Since avoiding Responsibility implies Coping, we see that avoiding negotiation and avoiding Responsibility are equivalent ideas. This means that TRP chart sheds light on the tricks people use to avoid negotiation. So, wherever Denial, Lay Blame, Justify, Shame, Quit, or Obligation are being *expressed* or *acted out* or *embodied,* you can rest assured that this is a reflection of an internal state that has not been negotiated, an internal state of tyranny and slavery, or war. All of this is going on within each *poorly integrated person* who is Coping as best he can, but Coping nonetheless.

We see in this idea of using tricks to avoid negotiation, a glimpse of the truly insidious nature of Coping. CA tells us that when we encounter an upset, TRP kicks in and the mind starts by offering up Coping mindsets. What this means is that the mind starts by offering *tricks to avoid Responsibility*. Negotiation and, by implication, Responsibility is extremely difficult and so the mind doesn't start there. It starts by looking for something easier, something that requires far less effort. It starts with Coping. Realizing that the mindset of Responsibility is always available, even when the internal logic of Coping insists that it isn't, the choice to embody Coping, the choice to act or speak from this mindset, is a choice to avoid Responsibility. In choosing to *accept* Coping as good enough to play out in the world, we make a choice that echoes Adam's choice to act contrary to God's decree. Adam, the Bible tells us, was not deceived by the serpent (1 Timothy 2:14). This means that he did what he did consciously. And then, having sinned, he immediately starts embodying Coping mindsets. Fear takes over (Genesis 3:10), expressed as Shame, and he tries to hide from God (Genesis 3:7). Then, when confronted, he immediately Blames his wife (Genesis 3:12).

This brings us to the consideration of "original sin." Before doing so, let's get it out of our heads that the fruit involved was an apple. An apple comes from an apple tree, but the tree that Adam and Eve ate from wasn't an apple tree. The Bible tells us specifically the tree was the "tree of knowledge of good and evil" (Genesis 2:9). This particular tree was the only tree that Adam and Eve were forbidden to eat from. We don't even have to ascribe any sort of *magical* properties to this tree in order for it to serve its intended purpose. The mere act of eating from this tree is an act of disobedience against God. Nothing more is required. The act of eating from the tree brings with it, the awareness of having done wrong. Evil, doing wrong when you know to do right, is implicit in the mere act of eating from this tree. Awareness of disobedience is the result.

Adam and Eve start off naive. They have no personal experience of having done anything wrong, no personal experience of having done anything evil, and so they lack the experiential knowledge of good and evil. The act of eating from the tree is an act, first of calling God's Word into question followed by an act of turning away from God, and finally of actively doing the opposite of what God instructed. This one act, then, is nothing short of rebellion, and once committed, Adam and Eve gain experiential knowledge of good and evil, having now committed evil. And, having been warned ahead of time that this was an act worthy of death, they become afraid of death and God simultaneously. And so, the fruit of this particular tree is the experiential knowledge of good and evil. From that point on, all of our choices are pregnant with the possibility of embodying either the adversarial or the heroic tendencies, but the fear of death and God act as barriers to the latter.

We can think, therefore, of original sin as the emergence of self-consciousness as a result of the evolutionary development of the physical capacity for self-consciousness, as JP does. This self-consciousness presents itself as fear of the threat of death of course, just as JP maintains. But this nascent fear of death is indistinguishable from the fear, the unhealthy fear, of God. God and death both share the same general category of the ultimate unknown. What's more, the personal experiential knowledge of evil comes with a sense of guilt, which compounds the problem because entering into the presence of God requires standing, in our nakedness, before God and our sense of God's holiness causes us to shrink even further from this idea.

> *It is a fearful thing to fall into the hands of the living God.*
>
> – Hebrews 10:31

> *This description of initial motivated decision and consequent dissolution seems to me to characterize the processes and "bifurcated" final state of moral (and, therefore, psychological) degeneration more accurately and potently than any purely "scientific" theory of psychopathology generated to date. Of course, we are at present unable to take our rationally-reduced selves seriously enough to presume a relationship between evil as a "cosmic force" and our petty transgressions and self-betrayals. We believe that in*

reducing the scope and importance of our errors, we are properly humble; in truth, we are merely unwilling to bear the weight of our true responsibility.

– Maps of Meaning

To have a preference for Coping, then, is an expression of an unwillingness to take on, or more accurately, to operate from Responsibility. And so, every time we take one of the shortcuts that Coping offers, we are literally *falling short* of the mark, which is what sin represents. We may Justify this by saying we don't feel like we have a choice, but that is Denial of the fact that we are always free to enter Responsibility, and an even deeper Denial of the fact that we don't want to. Responsibility is like stepping into the presence of God, which itself is like stepping into the light, and that light reveals our darkness, this evil within, the evil that we now know by experience but don't want to recognize within ourselves. And so we prefer to hide, to run from the light, rather than step into it. *And this is the condemnation, that light is come into the world, and men loved darkness rather than light, because their deeds were evil* (John 3:19).

Repentance

The way of life is described as beginning in metanoia, a word translated "repentance" by the [Authorized Version], which suggests a moralized inhibition of the "stop doing everything you want to do" variety. What the word primarily means, however, is a change of outlook or spiritual metamorphosis, an enlarged vision of the dimensions of human life.

– Maps of Meaning

JP is here quoting Northrop Frye. Frye comes close—very close—to the meaning of the Biblical idea of repentance, but like JP Frye misses the most significant aspect of Biblical repentance. There's something critical that's missing from this "definition." The missing element is none other than the

Protagonist that has been erased as a result of approaching the Bible from a psychological perspective. As we've just seen, the fall represents a transformation from a state of "naive innocence" to conscious awareness of mortality, which transformed our original disposition or attitude toward God from one in which there was no fear to one that is dominated by fear. Salvation is the "restoration" of our original internal attitude toward God. This restoration is itself a *spiritual metamorphosis* of the disposition of the heart toward God. It is a drastic "change of outlook" of a very precise nature. That is, this change of outlook, or paradigm shift, isn't just any change of outlook but a change of outlook with respect to God. If you miss this point you fail to comprehend the Biblical significance of repentance. Look, for instance, how the word is used in the book of Acts:

> *I have declared to both Jews and Greeks that they must **turn to** **God** in repentance and have faith in our Lord Jesus* (Acts 20:21).

> *First to those in Damascus, then to those in Jerusalem and in all Judea, and then to the Gentiles, I preached that they should repent and **turn to God** and demonstrate their repentance by their deeds* (Acts 26:20).

Ever since the emergence of self-consciousness, or the fall, our *natural response* to God causes us to think in a way that is backward or even upside-down with respect to Scriptural truth. Nowhere is that more clearly illustrated than in this idea of repentance. Most people think that Christ's death served to get God to change His attitude toward humanity. That is, most people think that Christ's sacrifice served to get God to "repent." Man's current antagonism toward God causes him to see God as the one who needs to turn around. We imagine that it is God's disposition toward man rather than man's disposition toward God that needs to change. That is what works is all about. But the Bible is clear: "God was in Christ reconciling the world to Himself" (2 Corinthians 5:19). Pay careful attention to what this verse is expressing. Reconciliation has a direction. The one doing the turning is the one being reconciled. This verse makes it clear that it is man who needs to be reconciled to God, and not God to man. It's man who needs to turn around.

Recall that the Bible is the story of a promise that God made within himself to resolve a problem that man could not resolve on his own. God's intention and attitude have been set from before the foundation of the world. And that intention is clear right from the beginning. Just consider that God sought out Adam and Even in the garden after the fall. What's more, we see symbolically depicted in fact that God clothes the two of them (Genesis 3:21), that God's disposition toward Adam and Eve is still benevolent even though they have rebelled against Him, a capital offense. We see in this act a foreshadowing of God's intention to clothe humanity "in Christ."

> For those of you who were baptized into Christ have been clothed with Christ.
>
> – Galatians 3:27

Repentance, like faith, is greatly misunderstood, again, primarily because our thinking is upside-down with respect to "sound doctrine." Our "sense of self" or ego sees statements about faith and repentance and sees within these ideas something that it can do to earn or merit right standing with God. What it fails to recognize, however, is that God "grants" (or doesn't grant) repentance (Acts 11:18, 2 Timothy 2:25) in much the same way that faith is a gift of God.

For whom did Christ die?

The Biblical ideas of grace and election are two sides of the same coin. These two doctrines provide us with clarity around the question of who precisely Christ died to redeem. JP tells us that *The New Testament has been traditionally read as a description of a historical event, which redeemed mankind, once and for all.* The historical event being referred to here is Christ's death. JP seems to accept the idea that the Bible teaches that Christ's death, this historical event, *redeemed **mankind** once and for all.* I can't begin to describe just how misleading this statement is, and in so many ways. There's a muddling of Biblical ideas in here that point the mind in the wrong direction. Yes, the New Testament is a description of this historical event. And yes, this event has something to do with the redemption of mankind. But the idea that Christ's death "redeemed mankind once and for all" paints an entirely incorrect picture.

What the Bible teaches about what the death of Christ accomplished is something I spent years exploring. It's far from straightforward and volumes have been written on the subject. Nevertheless, there is a clear and definitive, "dogmatic" position with respect to the question "for whom precisely did Christ die?" JP gives the impression that the Bible's answer to this question is that Christ died to redeem everyone, to redeem *mankind*. A careful reading of the Bible, however, makes it abundantly clear that this is not the case. If Christ's death did in fact secure the redemption of all of mankind, the distinction between those that are Christ's and those that are the devil's (John 8:44), between the wheat and the tares (Matthew 13:24-30), between sheep and the goats (Matthew 25:32), and the distinction between heaven and hell are all nullified, rendered meaningless.

Discrimination between those that are Christ's and those that aren't is as much a part of Christianity, as much a part of the process that the New Testament is a description of, as discriminating between points that are in the set and those that are outside of the set is a part of the process that reveals the Mandelbrot set. One of my heroes or mentors, Dr. Martyn Lloyd Jones,[15] expresses the idea succinctly: "Christianity is a very exclusive and dogmatic faith." https://youtu.be/-vbydx95tVQ?t=608

If you've enjoyed JP's lectures on the Bible, you might enjoy Lloyd Jones. In fact, if you really want to understand the "within the paradigm" (i.e., Biblical) lines of discrimination that delineate between a believer and a non-believer, I would recommend his *Studies in the Sermon on the Mount*. It's a Christian classic consisting of a compilation of sixty of his sermons

---

15   Martyn Lloyd-Jones. In Wikipedia. https://en.wikipedia.org/wiki/Martyn_Lloyd-Jones

that "unpack" Christ's Sermon on the Mount, focusing to a large extent on the question of what constitutes a true believer.

This idea of discriminating between those who are "in" and those who are "out," brings us to one of the most hated doctrines in the Bible, the doctrine of Sovereign Grace. This dogma states that, at the most fundamental level, the answer to the question of who is "in" and who is "out" rests entirely in a choice that God made prior to creation.[16] In the final analysis, this dogma maintains that God not only *picks* or determines who is in the set and who isn't but that this *selection* or, in Biblical terms, *"election"* took place before time came into being (Ephesians 1:4). If you've watched JP's series on the book of Genesis, you won't see him pause to acknowledge God's election in his discussion of Jacob and Esau, but to get an idea of how critical that "little bit" is, consider the words of Paul in Romans where we are told, in no uncertain terms, that God chose Jacob and rejected Esau:

> 6 ... *For they are not all Israel, which are of Israel: 7 Neither, because they are the seed of Abraham, are they all children: but, In Isaac shall thy seed be called. 8 That is, They which are the children of the flesh, these are not the children of God: but the children of the promise are counted for the seed. 9 For this is the word of promise, At this time will I come, and Sara shall have a son. 10 And not only this; but when Rebecca also had conceived by one, even by our father Isaac; 11 (For the children being not yet born, neither having done any good or evil, that the purpose of God according to election might stand, not of works, but of him that calleth;) 12 It was said unto her, The elder shall serve the younger. 13 As it is written, Jacob have I loved, but Esau have I hated.*

> – Romans 9:6-13

Look at how Paul spells it out for us. He points directly to the verse in Genesis (25:23) that precedes the birth of Jacob and Esau, before either one

---

16   See Romans 9.

had done anything "good or evil" and shows how God's choice had already been made. In drawing attention to the fact that God's choice occurred before Jacob and Esau had done anything, it emphasizes the fact that the choice was not based on anything "in" them. This dogma, as verse 11 makes clear, goes right to the heart of God's purpose and so this is definitely a dogma worth maintaining if the objective is to understand the Biblical narrative properly.

It may be worth thinking about the process that reveals the Mandelbrot set at this point. The set itself is infinite but the process is *deterministic*. That is, every given point will always either be in the set or outside the set. Even before the iterations are calculated the outcome can be thought of as already determined. The outcome isn't revealed until the process is enacted, but in a very real sense it is already determined or "known" in the same way that God knows those who are His.

Now, to be fair to JP, he does have an idea that closely mirrors the Biblical doctrine of election. He expresses this idea during one of his discussions with SH. SH asks JP what he means by God. JP answers by laying out a rough sketch of the most important or fundamental aspects or characteristics of the God that he believes in (https://youtu.be/h1oaSt60b0o?t=5098).

Within that context JP says that "God is what calls and what responds in the eternal call to adventure." It isn't hard to see the God of the Bible reflected in this statement when we make explicit something that lies just below the surface. This idea that God is what calls *and* what responds in the eternal call to adventure becomes ridiculous, even meaningless if God does not remain a free agent. What I mean by that is that that which calls is not obligated to call, not obligated to call any, and certainly not obligated to call all. By the same token, that which responds is under no obligation to respond to every call. That is, God may call some and not respond to that call. Implicit in JP's idea, then, is the Biblical idea: "For many are called but few are chosen" (Matthew 22:14). God is that which calls. God is that which responds to the call. And God does so according to His purpose, the purpose that will be discovered through this call, this eternal call to adventure.

Christ's death, then, did in fact secure redemption *once and for all*. But this redemption isn't the redemption of all of mankind individually. It secured the redemption of many but not all. "Even as the Son of man came not to be ministered unto, but to minister, and to give his life a ransom **for many**" (Matthew 20:28). "So Christ was once offered to bear the sins **of many**; and unto them that look for him shall he appear the second time without sin unto salvation" (Hebrews 9:28). In Revelation, we're told something about the reach or extent of this "many." *And they sang a new song, saying: "You are worthy to take the scroll, And to open its seals; For You were slain, And have redeemed us to God by Your blood Out of every tribe and tongue and people and nation"* (Revelation 5:9). Jesus himself makes it clear that the Father has given him people "out of the world." *I have manifested Your name to the men whom You have given Me out of the world. They were Yours, You gave them to Me, and they have kept Your word* (John 17:6). This verse paints a clear picture of God's election and Christ's *particular redemption*. "Particular redemption," that's the theological term for it. Another is "limited atonement." Regardless of the label, however, the idea is that the Bible teaches that the process of redemption is deterministic. And so, the historical event that the New Testament describes did in fact, once and for all, secure redemption but only for those it was intended, those chosen by God before the foundation of the world. The "entire set" of the elect throughout all time is what the Bible calls the Body of Christ or the Church, the Bride of Christ and it is specifically and only this group that Christ died to redeem:

> *Husbands, love your wives, even as Christ also loved the church, and gave himself for it.*

– Ephesians 5:25

.The Gospel

> *For I am not ashamed of the gospel of Christ: for it is the power*
> *of God unto salvation...*

– Romans 1:16

The *natural* response of a heart that is no longer innocent but knows its own guilt and *nakedness* is to turn away and run off in the opposite direction, like those points that are not in the Mandelbrot set. This disposition of the heart, which is ruled by fear, is the problem that man cannot fix himself because without divine revelation, without Scripture, he has no *structure of behavioral adaptation* for this particular situation. Fortunately, we do have Scripture to provide this *structure* and inform us about salvation, which, as we saw in our discussion of repentance, consists of a *spiritual metamorphosis* which alters the natural disposition of the heart with respect to God. As a result of this metamorphosis, the individual repents or does a 180-degree turn with respect to God, turning, as it were *to God*. The use of the word "metamorphosis" is helpful here because it highlights the internal transformation that a true change of heart constitutes. Not just that, but it also helps us to understand the means by which God enacts his plan of salvation. The means that God has chosen to produce this metamorphosis is a story, a seemingly foolish story, the Gospel. *For after that in the wisdom of God the world by wisdom knew not God, it pleased God by the foolishness of preaching to save them that believe* (1 Corinthians 1:21).

The Gospel is a story, a story within a story. The entirety of the Biblical narrative is the outer story. It provides the context which informs us of the nature of the problem that all of humanity is faced with. We must first understand the problem if we are to understand the solution, the inner story, the Gospel, which is why we've taken time to look into the nature of the Biblical *fall of man*. The loss of innocence that the fall represents isn't a trivial matter, either, because it means guilt, guilt before a holy God. As a result, this loss of innocence is equivalent to loss of right-standing before God. Denial of this guilt leaves the problem unaddressed. Recognition or acknowledgment of the guilt is, therefore, a prerequisite to genuine repentance. What's more, proper recognition of this guilt is far more than a mere mental ascent to dogma. It's a recognition of our nakedness and vulnerability, our helplessness before God. *To "know" nakedness—and to be shamed by it—is to understand exposure, weakness and vulnerability...To be unaware of nakedness—to lack "self-consciousness"—is to be much less troubled, but also—to be much less"* (MoM). To enter into God's presence with integrity requires a knowledge and deep awareness of our "nakedness," requires recognition that we are *not right* before God. Lack of this awareness is Denial of the reality of the situation.

> *There is nothing which is so utterly contrary to the whole teaching of the Bible as the assumption that anyone, and at any time, without any conditions whatsoever, may approach God... Man, by sin, has forfeited his right to approach God, and, indeed, were he left to himself he never would approach God.*
>
> –Ian Murray: *D. M. Lloyd-Jones, The Fight of Faith*

What primarily distinguishes Christianity (and Judaism) from most Oriental religions, it seems to me, is this revolutionary and prophetic element of confrontation with society (MoM). The Gospel confronts us with this reality and will not allow us to hide from it. Our sin cannot just be dismissed or ignored. *If we say that we have no sin, we deceive ourselves, and the truth is not in us* (1 John 1:8). It must be faced. We must *know* our nakedness before God. This nakedness is more than just weakness and vulnerability, however. It is also awareness of a heart that is *turned away* from God, a heart in rebellion against God. The Gospel demands honesty before God and this honesty starts with an admission of guilt, a recognition of our inability to save ourselves, to make ourselves right in the sight of God. Denial of this fact or worse, insistence in our innocence or our ability to earn God's favor, constitutes a spirit of opposition to God's Word and ultimately, opposition to or rebellion against God. Denial of the problem can only result in a failure to recognize the necessity of the solution, God's solution, the Lamb of God. The Bible is clear about this. The fall necessitates the death of Christ, which is why He is referred to as the *Lamb slain from the foundation of the world* (Revelation 13:8).

Repentance, which constitutes turning *to God*, requires the recognition that we are, in our natural state, *turned away from God*, guilty in his presence, and helpless to do anything about it. The heart that fails to see its own condition before God will never seek salvation, will never acknowledge the need for a savior, and will never genuinely repent. The soul that doesn't recognize its true state before God will never understand the substitutionary nature of Christ's work on the cross, that Christ wasn't *lifted up* on the cross (John 3:14) so that we can learn to imitate Him. The Gospel tells us that He was lifted up so that we could identify with him as our sacrifice, as having taken our place, paid the price for our sin. Biblical "identification with the hero" is first and foremost, identification with Christ as having taken our place. *For Christ also suffered once for sins, the just for the unjust, that He might bring us to God, being put to death in the flesh but made alive by the Spirit* (1 Peter 3:18).

The Bible is the story of man's inevitable fall from grace and God's promise to restore man to a state of right-standing with Himself. Both the problem and the solution were known to God before time began, before creation. Christ's death on the cross was substitutionary in nature, with Christ's death, once and for all, atoning for the sins of all those for whom His death was intended. So when Christ cries out "it is finished" (John 19:30), he is saying that God's promise had been officially ratified, sealed or signed in Christ's blood (Hebrews 9: 16-28). This is the "once and for all" aspect of redemption. But redemption must play itself out in time and in the hearts of individuals, and the Gospel is the means by which this is done. The Gospel, then, is a story intended to produce a paradigm shift, a radical transformation or metamorphosis consisting in a drastic change of outlook toward God.

The Gospel offers the *work of Christ* on the cross as the solution. God, in essence, says "This sacrifice is acceptable to Me and anyone who trusts in this sacrifice is accepted into My presence." *Therefore, brethren, having boldness to enter the Holiest by the blood of Jesus* (Hebrews 10:19). Salvation is entirely on God's terms. Through the Gospel, God extends this offer of restored right-standing in His presence, to anyone and everyone who *believes,* which is to say, accepts this sacrifice as not only sufficient but also as the only way to be made right with God. Merit has no place in God's plan of salvation as the very idea of merit denies the true nature of the problem, and denies the necessity of God's solution. Through the Gospel, God says, *I have sacrificed the ideal man for your sake, so that you can attain, re-attain right-standing with Me by accepting this sacrifice as the only cure for the disease* (Numbers 21:9). The Gospel is the story that makes the solution visible and it is the means that God uses to "open the eyes" of those He chooses to save (Romans 10:14).

The internal metamorphosis that constitutes repentance starts with a correct understanding of the problem and the problem is deeply personal as it reveals our individual wrong-standing in the sight of God. The metamorphosis of the individual begins when the heart recognizes its helpless, or *naked and vulnerable* state before God and sees, in Christ, God's own solution to this problem. The metamorphosis is complete when the individual accepts Christ's death on the cross as necessitated by his own sin and his heart responds in gratitude toward God. This is *turning to God.* The process of metamorphosis starts with a heart that actively runs from God and ends with a heart that is attracted to God, a heart that is filled with gratitude and love toward God. The process culminates not only in a heart that loves God but in a heart that understands the correct causal chain in this process. *We love Him because He first loved us* (1 John 4:19). The heart that has undergone this metamorphosis has done an about-face with respect to God and, along with Jonah, recognizes that from beginning to end "Salvation is of the LORD" (Jonah 2:9).

When I look at myself, I don't see how I can be saved.
But when I look at Christ, I don't see how I can be lost.

– Martin Luther

The Biblical narrative is the story of this inevitable problem that would befall mankind and that mankind would be helpless to resolve, and how God promised to intervene in the history of mankind in order to do just that. The Bible informs us of the nature of the problem and the Gospel provides us with God's solution. The offer of salvation goes out to "many" and the work of salvation, the metamorphosis of the individual's heart, is brought about when God uses this story to enlighten the individual's understanding (Ephesians 1:18). Along with this change in understanding comes a change of heart, such that the heart that once opposed God and His Word becomes filled with love and gratitude toward God. This is how salvation works at the level of the individual. This is God's plan of salvation with respect to the elect, individually over the course of history. The call goes out in the form of a story. God answers the call, awakening the individual who then responds, voluntarily, with gratitude. And the lifelong journey of genuine identification with the Hero begins.

Perhaps you're starting to see that the Bible is, at its most fundamental level, a love story between God and humanity, or at least a subset of humanity. There's more to this story than meets the eye, however. The doctrine of particular redemption hides something in plain sight, something that requires a slightly deeper look at God's plan of salvation in order to see. So we're going to do an about-face here. Having shown how JP is wrong about the New Testament being a description of *a historical event, which redeemed mankind, once and for all*, we're now going to show how he is right. To do this, however, we need to understand what the Bible means by "world."

I suspect most Westerners have a sense of how the Biblical narrative ends. Most likely, that sense is that God intends to destroy the world. There is, of course, an element of truth to this. God does intend to destroy the world but not in the way that the imagination automatically conjures up when processing those words, the word "world" especially. So we're going to explore what precisely the Bible means by *the world* when it speaks of God bringing about its destruction. Once we're clear on that, we'll be in the position to understand how the Bible can claim that Christ died to redeem the world, all of mankind, and that God intends to destroy the world. When correctly understood, we'll be able to see how the redemption of the Church is the means to achieving the greater objective, the salvation of mankind. That is, we'll be able to reconcile the seemingly incompatible ideas that God intends to destroy the world and that God's motivation for sending the redeemer was out of love for the world (John 3:16).

The World: Its destruction and salvation

You might be tempted to think that the world that God intends to destroy can be defined as everyone who is not one of the elect. This would be to define the world in terms of its inhabitants, the individuals in the world. The idea behind the word "world," however, is more sophisticated than that. It starts there, for sure, but it points to something deeper, something closer to the "spirit" or the "dynamic" of the group consisting of the non-elect.

We've been looking at the Biblical narrative through the lens of the individual. We've seen how the poorly integrated individual is split within himself and how he is powerless to fix himself. We've also seen how the individual prefers to avoid Responsibility and uses the Coping mindsets as tricks to avoid Responsibility. With this, we've laid the groundwork for correctly understanding the meaning of the word *world* within the context of that which the Bible says God intends to destroy.

Recall that a paradigm is like a game. Recall, also, that the Coping mindsets are like paradigms, which come with their own internal logic, or rules. Now, rather than thinking in terms of individuals, let's consider the problem statement in terms of groups.

> *The dialectic of metanoia and sin splits the world into the kingdom of genuine identity, presented as Jesus' "home," and a hell, a conception found in the Old Testament only in the form of death or the grave. Hell is that, but it is also the world of anguish and torment that man goes on making for himself all through history*

> – Maps of Meaning

Here JP, quoting Frye, identifies the two groups we are concerned with. One is characterized by genuine identity with Christ, which we've just looked at. The other is the one we are interested in here. The description of the second group is alluded to in the words, "the world of anguish and torment that man goes on making for himself all through history." This is a good starting point.

Consider, for a moment, a group of individuals who habitually embody Coping mindsets. What we know for sure about these individuals is that they are not solving or resolving problems but avoiding Responsibility. These individuals are playing a game. The internal logic of these Coping mindsets constitutes the rules of the game. What's more, we know that these individuals are "split" within themselves. It isn't hard to see that the internal dynamics of tyranny and slavery will spill out into the group. Except now, the dynamic isn't being played out between partial personalities within an individual but between individuals within the group. The dynamic is essentially the same, however, but now "visible" in the form of dominant individuals tyrannizing other individuals who play out the role of slaves.

The war within the individual breaks out into the group. *What causes fights and quarrels among you? Don't they come from your desires that battle within you?* (James 4:1) The result is a group that is governed by the internal dynamics of the poorly integrated individual. This, in turn, becomes a major problem, an insurmountable problem, because these rules, when enacted, become the governing, yet often invisible, rules of the group. And the *group* has a *mind* of its own. Once the group has internalized these rules, the dynamic becomes self-perpetuating as group members interact with each other, teaching each other how to Cope rather than how to operate from Responsibility. That is, the group that *embodies* this dynamic, animating the rules of the game, the game of Coping in this case, and the rules are "automatically" implicitly communicated to each of the group members. *"You modify me, I modify you, we both modify others, etc."* (MoM). The result is a group dynamic that is in open opposition to, or in rebellion against, God. The critical thing to understand here is that this group dynamic, the game itself has a life all its own. The individuals themselves are trapped within the game, within the group dynamic. What's more, this particular dynamic constitutes a degenerating or non-iterable game, a losing game. When we understand this, we are in a position to understand what the Bible means by "world."

In truth, the Bible uses the word "world" in different ways depending on context. We would be correct, for instance, in assuming that humanity itself is what the word world signifies in John 3:16, where the Bible says that God so loved the world (John 3:16). But that the world can also signify something closer to a dynamic Paul makes clear: *For we wrestle not against flesh and blood, but against principalities, against powers, against the rulers of the darkness of this world, against spiritual wickedness in high places* (Ephesians 6:12). In fact, wherever we see an expression of God's love and compassion towards *the world,* it is invariably humanity itself that is the object of that mercy. It would be nice to be able to say that wherever we see God's anger and wrath at *the world,* that it's primarily the dynamic, the game, and its rules, that are the object of this wrath; but the Bible isn't that simplistic and for good reason. But on that note, we should take care to observe that when God's anger is directed toward *the inhabitants of the world,* these individuals never constitute all of humanity and so we are better served thinking of them as representatives of the larger group and its dynamic, and they themselves as those who have *sold their souls to that group.* What's critical is that we recognize that a group comprised of individuals embodying the adversarial spirit, a group comprised of individuals embodying Coping (tyranny and slavery) rather than Responsibility (negotiation) will reinforce the rules of the game it is playing.

> *Group membership, social being, represents a necessary advance over childish dependence, but the spirit of the group requires its pound of flesh. Absolute identification with a group means rejection of individual difference: means rejection of "deviation," even "weakness," from the group viewpoint; means repression of*

individuality, sacrifice of the mythic fool—abandonment of the simple and insufficient "younger brother." The group, of course, merely feels that it is doing its duty by insisting upon such sacrifice; believes, with sufficient justification, that it is merely protecting its structure.

– Maps of Meaning

To those who have "sold their souls" to the group, however, the Word is indistinguishable from the enemy.

– Maps of Meaning

And be not conformed to this world: but be ye transformed by the renewing of your mind, that ye may prove what is that good, and acceptable, and perfect, will of God.

– Romans 12:2

A Christian is not to conform to this world, which is to say to the funda-mental *patterns of action, imagination, and thought* of this current age. We know that the *god of this age* is *the adversary,* and so this is a clear directive not to embody the dominant tendency of the world dynamic or spirit, the adversarial tendency. *The god of this age has blinded the minds of unbelievers, so that they cannot see the light of the gospel that displays the glory of Christ, who is the image of God* (2 Corinthians 4:4). Thinking along these lines, of group dynamics rather than just individual behavior, opens up a way of understanding how God could simultaneously destroy the world and save humanity.

The other historical event: The marriage of the lamb

Perhaps the New Testament has been traditionally read as a description of a historical event, but it can more accurately be said that it is a description of two historical events, one in the past, the death of Christ, and the other in the future. Traditionally, the future event is referred to as the return of

Christ. Having looked briefly at the beginning of the Biblical narrative, the problem statement, and the middle of the narrative, the process of salvation being worked out in time through the Gospel, it's time to turn our attention to the end of the story.

> *11 Seeing then that all these things shall be dissolved, what manner of persons ought ye to be in all holy conversation and godliness, 12 Looking for and hasting unto the coming of the day of God, wherein the heavens being on fire shall be dissolved, and the elements shall melt with fervent heat? 13 Nevertheless we, according to his promise, look for new heavens and a new earth, wherein dwelleth righteousness.*
>
> – 2 Peter 3:11-13

A quick reading of these verses gives the impression that God intends to completely destroy everything. But, we're interested in something deeper than just a first impression, so let's turn our attention to this idea of the *dissolution* of the current *world* coupled with the idea of the establishment of a new *world*. These ideas should sound extremely familiar. They mirror, almost perfectly, JP's idea that "Movement from one schema to another... presupposes dissolution... not mere addition (presupposes a "qualitative" shift, not a "quantitative" shift)." This pattern is represented rather abstractly, however. So let's look at a description of the same pattern in the Book of Exodus:

> *The biblical story of Exodus is properly regarded as archetypal (or paradigmatic or foundational) by psychoanalytic and religious thinkers alike, because it presents an example of psychological and social transformation that cannot be improved upon. It emerged as a product of imagination and has been transformed by constant collective retelling and reworking into an ultimately meaningful form that applies politically, economically, historically, personally, and spiritually, all at the same time. This is the very definition of literary depth—something that reaches its apogee in certain forms*

*of ancient, traditional stories. The fact of that depth means that such accounts can be used diversely as a meaningful frame for any process of profound change experienced by any individual or society (**stable state, descent into chaos, reestablishment of stability**), and can lend that process multidimensional reality, context, powerful meaning, and motivation.*

– Beyond Order

We gain insights into the event that Peter is describing by thinking in terms of a "process of profound change" that starts with a stable state, is followed by a descent into chaos, which is followed by the reestablishment of stability. One world, the current "evil" world (Galatians 1:4), will be dissolved and a new world, a world "wherein dwelleth righteousness" is to be established. Given everything we've covered to this point, we could express these ideas using only slightly different terminology. The current evil world is the world under, or ruled by, the dynamic of Coping. The age to come, the world in which righteousness dwells, is the world under, or ruled by, the dynamic of Responsibility. The transformation of the world that Peter describes constitutes just such a *profound change*, a qualitative change, a change in the governing dynamic, or ruling "spirit." This qualitative change is nothing less than the dissolution of, the destruction of the present world, and the establishment of a new world. It's worth noting that this transformation, like the transformation of the individual apprentice, is the result of *heat and pressure,* only now we're talking about the same process operating at a very different scale. JP compares the heat and pressure of the apprenticeship process to the heat and pressure needed to turn carbon into diamond. Well, Peter is using essentially the same analogy, only Peter's is not generally recognized for what it is.

Let's turn our attention to the second historical even that the New Testament is a description of, only let's focus on one particular aspect of that event, the marriage of the Lamb to His Bride. Christ's work on the cross was specifically to *purchase* or *redeem* his Bride: *Be shepherds of the church of God, which he bought with his own blood* (Acts 20:28). Read the Gospels and you'll find Jesus himself speaking with anticipation of this event. And in the Book of Hebrews, we are given a glimpse of what this event meant to Him. *For the joy set before him he endured the cross, scorning its shame..."* Christ endured the cross in anticipation of the joy of this event, when Christ and his Bride would be united. It should come as no surprise, then, to find that this event constitutes the climactic event of the Biblical narrative.

> *9 And there came unto me one of the seven angels which had the seven vials full of the seven last plagues, and talked with me, saying, Come hither, I will shew thee the bride, the Lamb's wife.*
>
> *10 And he carried me away in the spirit to a great and high mountain, and shewed me that great city, the holy Jerusalem, descending out of heaven from God, 11 Having the glory of God: and her light was like unto a stone most precious, even like a jasper stone, clear as crystal; 12 And had a wall great and high, and had twelve gates, and at the gates twelve angels, and names written thereon, which are the names of the twelve tribes of the children of Israel; 13 On the east three gates; on the north three gates; on the south three gates; and on the west three gates. 14 And the wall of the city had twelve foundations, and in them the names of the twelve apostles of the Lamb.*
>
> – Revelation 21:9-14

Here we have a symbolic dramatization of the event we've been speaking of. These verses provide a symbolic representation of the establishment of the world in which righteousness dwells. This new world, the *holy Jerusalem*, descends from God. God sets it on earth and then dwells there. *And the city had no need of the sun, neither of the moon, to shine in it: for the glory of God did lighten it, and the Lamb is the light thereof* (Revelation 21:23). What's critical to note is that this city that is descending from heaven represents the *Lamb's bride*. The ideas are symbolically joined together in these verses; the union of Christ with His bride and the establishment of this new world are inseparable. And so, the dissolution of the world and the establishment of a new world can be clearly seen even if represented mostly symbolically.

This marriage is meant to be taken as more than just a simple metaphor, however. The idea that's developed in the Bible is that this event consists of something like the consummation of wedding vows. There's an element of *physical union* that is meant to be taken seriously. Somehow, this as yet future event consists of Christ being actually *united* with His bride. Now that the process that the New Testament is a description of has been made explicit and now that we understand how this Process, Christ, is embodied in us, in the form of TRP, we can see how Christ can be *united* with, let's say, a critical mass of people. This union of Christ with His bride is the marriage of the Lamb, but it is also the death of the current dynamic and the establishment of a new dynamic. This, of course, implies that there will be mass adoption of this process when this event begins. Once begun, the old dynamic will fall from its position of dominance as a new dynamic establishes dominance. "And they shall not teach every man his neighbour, and every man his brother, saying, Know the Lord: for all shall know me, from the least to the greatest" (Hebrews 8:11). This is also the salvation of the world, as chaos is relegated to a subordinate role and flow is re-established on earth.

> *1 And he shewed me a pure river of water of life, clear as crystal, proceeding out of the throne of God and of the Lamb. 2 In the midst of the street of it, and on either side of the river, was there the tree of life, which bear twelve manner of fruits, and yielded her fruit every month: and the leaves of the tree were for the healing of the nations. 3 And there shall be no more curse: but the throne of God and of the Lamb shall be in it; and his servants shall serve him: 4 And they shall see his face; and his name shall be in their foreheads. 5 And there shall be no night there; and they need no candle, neither light of the sun; for the Lord God giveth them light: and they shall reign for ever and ever.*

–Revelation 22:1-5

We should take note that the narrative comes full circle. The tree of Life, the other *special* tree from the garden, is brought back into the narrative. This brings us all the way back to the fall and man's banishment from the garden when God cut-off man's access to this tree as a consequence of his rebellion against God (Genesis 3:22-23). At the end of the narrative, once God's plan of salvation has played itself out fully in history and man's right-standing in the sight of God has been restored, access to this tree is also restored, symbolizing man's restoration to a state of grace, only this state of grace is no longer naive innocence but informed maturity. And, on this note, we should take care to observe that the leaves of the tree serve a particular purpose, the healing of the nations. This *healing of the nations* implies that God does not, in the end, *wipe out* humanity in the process of destroying the world.

While we've only just scratched the surface, we've touched on enough significant points to be able to connect all of the dots together. We now have a clear picture of the nature of the problem, man's loss of right-standing in the sight of God as self-consciousness emerged and man came to associate the unknown, and the Ultimate Unknown, with the threat of death. This threat is so frightening that man turns in fear and as a result, turns away from God. But God, valuing His relationship with his creation, determined to redeem mankind from its captivity to fear. The Biblical narrative, then, is the story of God's plan of redemption playing itself out through time, from the fall all the way to the future event in which mankind's right-standing with God is restored when Christ is *united* with humanity, symbolized by the marriage of the Lamb.

Christians may balk at such ideas, but they should be careful not to repeat the mistake made by the Jews of Christ's day. Christians accept that the Jews failed to recognize the coming of the Messiah. Christians also recognize that the transition from the Old Testament to the New Testament constitutes movement from one paradigm to another. This means they understand that, for the Jews, this required a paradigm shift, a paradigm shift that most Jews of the time were unable to make. They especially couldn't wrap their heads around God extending his plan of salvation beyond the Jewish nation to the Gentiles. Paul speaks to this very problem in Romans 9. He opens that chapter with an expression of the extreme sorrow that he felt as he witnessed *his people* being left behind as they rejected the Gospel. The primary reason the Jews couldn't shift paradigms, of course, is that the

Jews had too particular an expectation of what the coming of the Messiah would look like. Because what presented itself didn't match the expectation, it was rejected. The return of Christ promises to be a similar event, only this time it's the Christians that are in danger of being *left behind* as a result of too particular an expectation of what Christ's return "should" look like.

Christians, all true Christians, look forward to the return of Christ, but the ideas that they hold about what that's *supposed* to look like may very well blind them from seeing the event when it takes place. Consider, for example how Christians expect the return of Christ in physical form and how Jesus himself warned against thinking in such terms in Matthew 24, where he says specifically: *At that time if anyone says to you, 'Look, here is the Messiah!' or, 'There he is!' do not believe it"* (v. 23). What's more, in the same context, Jesus tells us that *For as lightning that comes from the east is visible even in the west, so will be the coming of the Son of Man* (v. 27). Up until just recently, with the emergence of the internet and the recognition that information can "go viral," we haven't had a way of making sense of such statements. But now we do.

The Biblical narrative ends with the "Revelation" of Christ. This has traditionally been read as the return of Jesus, but it can more accurately be understood as Christ being made visible. This is the emergence of what Christ represents as it transforms from something that is understood only implicitly, into something that is understood explicitly. And that brings us back to JP's thinking about the New Testament being a description of a process *that, if enacted, could bring about the establishment of peace on earth.* The problem, as JP informs us, is that *this process cannot yet really be said to be "consciously"—that is, explicitly—understood.* There's a very similar Biblical idea, an idea that the Apostle Paul expresses to the Church in Corinth: *9 For we know in part and we prophesy in part. 10 But when that which is perfect has come, then that which is in part will be done away* (1 Corinthians 13:9-10). In the Bible, the word "perfect" generally signifies "complete" or "mature," and not perfect in the sense that we generally use it now. This is consistent with the way in which an idea emerges from the shadows of implicit knowledge into the light of the explicitly declared. So, it's significant then, that it is specifically *knowledge and prophesy* that are currently *incomplete* or not fully *mature* or *in part.* Paul is telling us, in no uncertain terms, that our current understanding, which is only partial, allows us to see only a blurry reflection of reality (1 Corinthians 13:12). But Paul goes further by telling us that a better, more complete, mature, which is to say *perfect* understanding is coming and when it arrives, it will *do away* with our current imperfect understanding. And that sounds suspiciously like movement from one paradigm, or schema, to another.

The marriage of the Lamb represents a dramatic global paradigm shift as the "god of this age" Satan, which is the dynamic of this current "evil" world, is replaced by a different dynamic, a dynamic that emerges from individuals on mass "enacting" the process that the New Testament is a description of. And now that this process has been rendered explicit in TRP, there is nothing preventing this from taking place. What's more, and at the risk of sounding insane, now that I've recognized or "seen" Christ, the second historical event that the New Testament is a description of has officially begun. And this brings us back to our Protagonist. As I write these words, I'm all too aware of how insane I sound, even to myself, when I assert that this "revelation of Christ" will result in a global transformation of the dominant dynamic in the world. Nevertheless, I am convinced that my *reading* of the Bible is correct and that this has been God's plan all along, to reveal Himself through Christ and to lead humanity to this transformation and restored right-standing with Him.

> *Eye has not seen, nor ear heard, Nor have entered into the heart of man The things which God has prepared for those who love Him.*
>
> –1 Corinthians 2:9

The treasure symbolically represented

Let's revisit the representation of my "lens of perception" that we examined in the previous chapter. More specifically, let's pause to consider the symbolic representation of JP's conception of Christ that appears on the third layer in the position that corresponds to the Eucharist on the first layer.

Image 9: Symbolic representation of JP's conception of Christ

Let's look at the symbols in this image and recall what each one represents. First, of course, is the Mandelbrot set, which represents the "set" of all individuals through all time who are "in Christ," which of course is the "body of Christ." This set, which is infinitely deep, echoes back to God's promise to Abraham that his "spiritual" descendants would be "as numerous as the stars in the sky and as the sand on the seashore" (Genesis 22:1). The Mandelbrot set, therefore, is a fitting update to the Eucharist which is also a symbolic representation of the body of Christ. The Uroboros, as we've made clear already, represents the iterative feedback process that was used to generate the Mandelbrot set. The diamond that is set within the serpent's head echoes back to the words that God spoke to the serpent immediately after the fall. Foreshadowing the coming of Christ, God says to the serpent: "he will crush your head, and you will strike his heel" (Genesis 3:15). The crushing of the serpent's head is represented by the enlightened understanding and the clarity that comes through TRP and makes visible Satan's "tricks" (2 Corinthians 2:11) for getting people to abdicate Responsibility and yield to the adversarial tendency. So, the diamond "planted within" the serpent's head depicts Satan's defeat as his tricks to get us to avoid Responsibility are laid bare for all to see. TRP allows us to see inside the devil's mind, as it were, and recognize just how subtle a thing Coping is. By shining the light on what differentiates between an iterative game and a degenerating game, we now know how to reject the call of the adversarial tendency and how to follow the call of the heroic principle. But this image isn't meant to be seen only as an aggregate of independent pieces.

Together, these symbols are best understood as a ring, a wedding ring to be more precise. And here we see where JP fails to see the big picture because he's taken the Protagonist out of His own Book. This ring represents the covenant relationship between Christ and His bride. God has entered into a covenant relationship, first with Christ, promising Him a bride worthy of His sacrifice. On an individual basis, God has been redeeming individual hearts and entering into a covenant relationship with them. Abraham, Isaac, and Jacob are all examples of God choosing to enter into a covenant relationship with these individuals. God calls to each individual and responds to that call within each individual such that that person repents and enters voluntarily into the relationship. With the Mandelbrot set representing the Bride of Christ and the Uroboros and diamond representing the wedding band, this symbol represents God's promise to bring this sacred union into being.

This second historical event described in the New Testament, this wedding, this union of Christ with humanity is what the first historical event described in the New Testament guaranteed *once and for all*. History then, human history, has been marching steadily towards this event ever since the fall. Those who are Christs have been "looking for and hastening the coming of the day of God" or, anticipating this second event ever since the first took place (2 Peter 3:12).

The only question, then, is will you put on the ring? Will you refuse to embody the adversarial tendency and cease to act or speak from any of the Coping mindsets? Will you resolve to operate, which is to say, speak and act only from Responsibility? Will you follow Christ? Will you enter into a covenant relationship with God? Will you put on the ring and never take it off? You may think you know the answer to this question, but the next upset will inform you about the true state of your heart. Your resolve will be tested, not just by the next upset but by the one after that and the one after that until you demonstrate that you are in fact in a stable orbit around God or that you prefer to run away, to run off to infinity.

5.
ASCENT: A PERSONAL LETTER TO JORDAN B. PETERSON

Thanksgiving weekend 2022.

Jordan,

I suspect you don't remember me, but you and I have met, briefly, a few months ago during your *Beyond Order* book tour. I came on stage during the photo op portion of the event. I shook your hand, looked you in the eye, and thanked you for your help. What's more, that night when I stepped on stage, I had with me an envelope on which I'd printed the words:

> *Testament has been traditionally read as a description of a historical event, which redeemed mankind, once and for all; it might more reasonably be considered the description of a process that, if enacted, could bring about the establishment of peace on earth.*
>
> The problem is, however, that this process cannot yet really be said to be "consciously"—that is, explicitly—understood.

The envelope itself contained a copy of Christopher Avery's The Responsibility Process chart. The envelope also held a USB thumb drive containing a draft of this book. You'll have no memory of this, since the envelope never made it into your hands, but you may yet recall our very brief interaction.

Let me see if I can jar your memory a bit. How many people come on stage during the photo op but don't get their picture taken with you? Someone coming on stage and not getting their picture taken with you should stand out as anomalous behavior and so you may yet have some recollection of meeting me. Unlike most other people, when I shook your hand I made it clear that I wasn't there for the photo op but simply to thank you, which I did. But I did more than just thank you.

As you can probably guess, that envelope was meant for you. In fact, my original intention was to give you a very brief outline of how I came to discover an explicit declaration of this process that the New Testament describes before handing you the envelope. Just before the photo op, however, there was an announcement to the effect that participants were not to present you with any gifts and that we shouldn't take time to share stories with you.

I watched a number of people who, like me, had brought something along to give to you. What I observed gave me cause for concern that my envelope might simply be set aside and never opened by you. Given the importance of what I had to share with you I considered breaking the rules, but instead I chose to ask you to give me a couple of minutes of your time after the event. I didn't just ask you for your time, however; I offered you something in exchange for those two minutes. More specifically, I offered you two things in exchange for your time and it's precisely what I offered you that I think should make the memory come to the surface. After all, how many people come on stage to offer you a "truly unforgettable story" coupled with a "priceless gift." Those were my exact words, and I'd chosen them carefully. I expected, for instance, that that you would recognize the significance of my use of the phrase "unforgettable story" given the way that you use the phrase in *Beyond Order,* and it appeared, at least at first, that you did.

You seemed very emphatic about wanting to hear from me when you agreed to give me those two minutes. So, having secured a verbal agreement from you, I felt certain that I would have the opportunity tell my story and to present you with the envelope. I went back to my seat joyfully where my wife and I enjoyed the remainder of the event. Unfortunately, the event ran late and came to a rather abrupt end. You were rushed off stage and, from what I can see, never gave me another thought. And so, if you don't remember meeting me it's likely because I never really got a chance to say anything to you.

I can't begin to tell you how much that lost opportunity cost me. I went up on that stage believing that once I'd had the opportunity to talk to you that it would mean that I wouldn't have to travel the final grueling "mile" of my journey alone. I'd like to give you an idea of just how much it cost me to place my trust in that verbal agreement that night, and so, I'm going to provide you with an outline of the "ascent to the surface" and the part that you played in that ascent. Within that context, I think you'll be able to appreciate the impact that watching you disappear back stage had on me that night.

Stage 1: The first six years

The year 2012 was an especially significant year for me. As we've already seen, that's the year that I encountered "my dead father" within the belly of the beast at the bottom of that nihilistic void. That initial encounter with The Responsibility Process marks the beginning of my ascent back to the surface. And, while I still didn't have any idea about what I was doing, I did have a sense that I was embarking on a very long ascent that would take all I had to successfully reach the summit.

I'd first gotten this "sense" of what was coming shortly before going to Europe and standing in the Stanza of the Signatura. This trip to Europe would start in Rome and then move to Paris, and knowing that I might never again find myself in France, I decided to do something that would certainly have been on my bucket list if I had such a list. That something was to cycle up one of the most famous climbs of the Tour de France, Alpe d'Huez.[17] If you've ever ridden a bike up a steep hill, you'll appreciate just how challenging a 13-km ride up a slope that has an average gradient of

---

17   Alpe d'Huez. In Wikipedia. https://en.wikipedia.org/wiki/Alpe_d%27Huez

8.1% might be. For me, it was more than just a physical challenge, though. For me it was symbolic of another ascent that I felt was just around the bend.

The ascent up Alpe d'Huez has 21 hairpin bends, and for that reason reminds me of something from *Beyond Order*:

> *Aim at something profound and noble and lofty. If you can find a better path along the way, once you have started moving forward, then switch course. Be careful, though; it is not easy to discriminate between changing paths and simply giving up. (One hint: if the new path you see forward, after learning what you needed to learn along your current way, appears more challenging, then you can be reasonably sure that you are not deluding or betraying yourself when you change your mind.) In this manner, you will zigzag forward. It is not the most efficient way to travel, but there is no real alternative, given that your goals will inevitably change while you pursue them, as you learn what you need to learn while you are disciplining yourself.*

Despite having trained as well as I could, having never faced a climb of this magnitude before, I had no way of knowing whether or not I could make it to the top. What I felt, however, is that I had to. Somehow the outcome of this climb seemed linked to the outcome of the invisible climb I knew would immediately follow. Of course, what I didn't know at the time was that this ascent out of the abyss that I'd jumped into would take ten years and would be every bit as challenging as the climb up Alpe d'Huez. Unlike this physical climb, however, where I knew how long it was and where the finish line was drawn, the climb out of the abyss came with the additional challenge of not knowing where the summit lay or how to get there. The path out of the abyss, like the path up Alpe d'Huez, was a zigzag, an extremely steep and unrelenting zigzag, a zigzag that would eventually lead me here, to the writing of this book and this "conclusion." But I had no way of knowing any of this at the time.

Motivation

I've only just begun to fully appreciate the role or the part that motivation plays in MoM. In fact, the word "motivation," in one form or another, appears over two-hundred times within the text. Seeing as motivation plays such an important role in your thinking, I thought it would only be fitting to center this chapter around motivation. More precisely, we're going to examine the various stages of motivation that drove me forward during the ascent back to the surface.

It starts with my interaction with CA. After the lecture I went up to shake his hand and thank him. I'm sure that he could see just how depressed I was at the time. Nevertheless, when I went up to shake his hand, I'd already determined that I wanted to live from this motivational state he called Responsibility. We spoke for only a minute or two, and the only thing that I remember from the conversation was the one piece of advice that he offered. That advice was simply to get clear about what I wanted.

What I wanted

This may sound strange, but he couldn't have given me a more challenging homework assignment. My life as a Christian had consisted, to a large extent, on a disciplined willingness to sacrifice what I wanted for what God wanted. As a Christian, my attitude had been, "not My will, but Yours, be done" (Luke 22:42). This was my prayer, though it often took a slightly different form. For instance, there was one prayer in particular, a prayer that I prayed regularly even though it filled me with fear just to hear myself utter the words. This prayer generally went something like, "Father, I am yours. Do with me as you please." Say those words slowly and mean them and I don't know if there's a more frightening prayer that can be uttered. This, after all, is just the sort of prayer that led Jesus to the cross. And so, every time I prayed this prayer I was reminded not only of the cross but also of those mentioned at the end of Hebrews 11, or the ordeals that the prophets went through, etc., etc. Regardless of how frightening it was to utter such words, I still did it, and I did so regularly and consistently over the period of my apprenticeship.

> *I beseech you therefore, brethren, by the mercies of God, that you present your bodies a living sacrifice, holy, acceptable to God, which is your reasonable service.*

— Romans 12:1

I had disciplined myself to put what I wanted second, a distant second, behind God's will. Because of this, the idea of focusing on what I wanted was, to me, a very foreign idea, one that would take me some time to get clear about.

Getting clear about what I wanted

I took CA's advice to heart and started thinking along the lines of what I wanted. While he hadn't said anything about prioritizing what I wanted, I discovered for myself that getting clear about what I wanted required not only identifying what I wanted but becoming clear about what I wanted *most*. So, at first I thought about what I wanted for myself. As a Christian, I'd sacrificed my financial future by giving 10% of my income to the Church, leaving me with no personal savings (Matthew 6:19). Making up for this deficit was high on my list of priorities, but there was something else, something new that made me look beyond myself. The something new came in the form of grandchildren. Grandchildren altered my perspective such that I found myself considering not only what I wanted for my future but what I wanted for their future.

There was something exceptionally troubling for me, however, when I considered my grandchildren's future. You see, when I "awoke as if from a Christian dream" I woke up in what appeared to me to be a Christian nightmare. What I mean by that is that when I experienced the death of God, I woke up in a culture that seemed to me to be playing out a self-fulfilling prophecy. The culture, it seemed to me, was saturated with a belief that the Bible taught that God was going to bring about an apocalyptic ending to life on earth. I no longer believed in God or that the Bible was the Word of God, so I was very concerned about how a culture will behave if it thinks that its most fundamental story teaches that God intends to bring about the complete and utter destruction of the world. It seemed to me that any culture that believes such a story is guaranteed to be marching toward its own destruction, and it seemed to me that I saw ample signs that we were accelerating down that path. This frightened me with respect to my own future, but it terrified me with respect to my grandchildren's future and the future of their entire generation.

As I continued this process of getting clear about what I wanted, I learned, by experience, that sacrifice plays a huge part. The things that I wanted were many, and as soon as I'd generated a list of what I wanted most, the items on the list began to fight for motivational influence or power. I experienced enough of these internal battles to become familiar with the pattern. Two things that I wanted would present themselves, usually accompanied by confusion. They would compete for my affection, as it were. This competition was emotionally upsetting, but it would persist until I reached a clear and unequivocal conclusion about which I would sacrifice for the other if I could have just one of them.

By analogy, this process of figuring out what I wanted constituted the first leg of the ascent. By the time I'd reached the first *hairpin bend*, I'd gotten clarity on that front. I think you would call this exercise getting my value hierarchy in order. Regardless, when I was done, I was clear about my number one priority, the thing I wanted above all others, the thing I would sacrifice everything to attain. That thing came in the form of a problem, a problem that I found myself picking up as a result of this exercise. The problem, in a nutshell, was this self-fulfilling prophecy that my culture was unconsciously enacting. My objective was to prevent this pattern from playing itself out to its logical conclusion. That's the problem that I took responsibility for and what motivated me to exert the effort required by the ascent.

In my mind, the physical ascent up Alpe d'Huez served as a symbolic representation of this mythological ascent. So I'm going to bounce back and forth between the two, mapping one to the other, in order to help give the mythological ascent more substance, which is to say a "form." The following image then not only represents the first leg of the climb up Alpe d'Huez, but simultaneously represents the first leg of the ascent back to the surface.

Image 10: Leg one of the ascent up Alpe d'Huez[18]

18 VerTdeTerre, CC BY-SA 3.0 <http://creativecommons.org/licenses/by-sa/3.0/>, via
Wikimedia Commons https://upload.wikimedia.org/wikipedia/commons/1/1e/Lacets_
AlpedHuez.jpg https://commons.wikimedia.org/wiki/File:Lacets_AlpedHuez.jpg

Faith

Taking responsibility for a problem entails taking ownership of the problem. So I determined that I would both "solve" this problem and bring about its solution, or go to my grave trying. The process of becoming clear about what I wanted lead me to the problem and I decided *make this problem my own and to work diligently for its solution*. From what I could see, this was the most critical issue of our time, and yet no one in their right mind would take responsibility for solving this problem. What that meant to me was that I couldn't expect that anyone else would take responsibility for it. As I saw it, either I took responsibility for this or no one would, which is to say, the problem would be left to play itself out to its logical conclusion. The thought of doing nothing and simply watching this play out, haunted me.

I wasn't ignorant of the magnitude of the problem, though. I knew full well that I was picking up an impossible problem, a problem for which it was completely unreasonable to believe that there was a solution, much less that a single individual could be capable of bringing such a solution into being. There was one more factor at play here, though, and that was The Responsibility Process. At that time I felt that this particular problem constituted the perfect problem to use as a test of TRP.

What I mean by that is that I approached TRP with a certain amount of scepticism. CA had described this motivational state he called Responsibility as "Owning your ability and power to create, choose, and attract."[19] I had a lot of issues with this description. As you'll recall, I was completely nihilistic and faithless when I ran into CA. The idea of owning your power to attract struck me as overly nebulous and even mystical. Nevertheless, I realized that a correct understanding of CA's conception of Responsibility would come only through practice. So it's TRP that lead me to identifying the problem I wanted to solve, and it's TRP that became my path forward.

---

19   This has evolved through the years. As I recall, it was simply "Owning your power to attract" when I first encountered TRP.

In all honesty, when I first started out, I thought CA was wrong. I didn't believe in anything even remotely resembling any "power to attract." The idea that a person's subjective attitude could somehow have an effect on the external world struck me as impossible. If it were true, it meant that the Universe itself had to be so constituted as to "partner with" the individual. This idea was a bit too close to the idea of God for my liking, but it seemed to be part of this process, so I decided I would go along in order to discover the truth for myself.

Even considering all of this, as I started this ascent, I didn't possess faith of any kind. I didn't, for instance, believe that I could resolve this problem or even have faith that the problem could in fact be resolved by anyone. I certainly didn't possess faith in my ability to attract a solution to this impossible problem I'd decided to shoulder. All I knew for sure was that I wanted the problem solved and that, at a minimum, I was willing to give it my best shot. The outcome didn't matter as much as the sincere effort.

Faith cannot be manufactured. As a result, I started the ascent more or less doomed to fail. But then, I came to the second hairpin bend of the ascent and that's when faith "manifested" itself within me. I remember it distinctly because it consisted of an experience like nothing I'd ever encountered before. It came soon after reading Robert Greene's *The 48 Laws of Power*. Robert Greene (RG) articulated an idea in *The 48 Laws of Power* that struck me as particularly applicable to my objective. The idea had to do with the nature of power and the way in which it could be "manufactured." In that context, RG talks about the mastery of something as a source of power. Through this idea, I was reminded of the fact that I had developed a mastery of the Bible during my days as a Christian. This reminder, or whatever you want to call it, somehow triggered something deep within me that resulted in a visceral experience that literally felt like a million little switches were being toggled inside my mind, inside my being. I could "feel" these switches like were a complex maze of dominoes falling in a chain reaction, inside my head. The sensation that came with this experience lasted for over 24 hours, and probably closer to 36.

Even as I could feel the dominos falling, I had an intuitive sense of what was going on. It was as if RG's ideas had reached in and given my sub-conscious the "hint" that it needed in order to believe that a solution was possible. Once that idea had become fixed, as it were, it was as if it triggered a complete rearranging of the physical circuits in my mind. The experience was so real that it seemed to me that I could hear the clicking they made as circuits that had previously been closed opened and open circuits closed. When it was over, what remained was a sense that the problem wasn't in fact insurmountable. Something inside of me now believed a solution was possible and so, once I'd rounded the second hairpin bend, I did so with an unshakeable faith that the problem could be solved even though I didn't know how and I also didn't know, with any certainty, that I could solve it. But knowing that it could be solved was all the motivation I needed to continue the ascent.

Not enough

The first six years of what would eventually turn out to be a ten-year ascent corresponds approximately to hairpin bend 13 of the Alpe d'Huez climb. In the physical climb, this corresponds to a very disconcerting realization that dawned on me at about that point. The realization was that it was now taking everything I had to maintain enough momentum to keep moving forward. Relaxing my pace, even slightly, came with the risk of grinding to a halt, and I knew that if I stopped, I'd likely not be able to get going again. Taking a break was out of the question, as it would constitute failure to accomplish what I'd set out to do, which was to climb this mountain in a single, unbroken effort. But the realization that I couldn't afford to slow down at all terrified me, because it meant that I was no longer able to reach down to grab my water bottle.

When riding up a steep incline like this, your legs do the bulk of the work but you also rely very heavily on your arms, which pull on the handlebars in order to allow you to push harder on the pedals. Letting go of the handlebars, even just one hand, meant not being able to pull with as much force because pulling on just one side of the handlebars makes riding in a straight line nearly impossible. Letting go of the handlebars meant my legs would have to push harder if I wasn't going to stall, but my legs were no longer capable of producing that kind of force. So I was struck with the realization that I would have to complete the climb without water, and this thought was daunting.

Six tenths of the way up the mythological ascent, which is to say six years into this process, I reached a corresponding realization. Throughout the first six years, my primary focus was twofold; I contended with TRP at a very personal level while also taking whatever steps forward I could with respect to the problem I'd taken on. One of these steps forward consisted of something that by this time I honestly thought I would never do, and that was to revisit the Bible. As a result, by the time I'd been ascending for six years, I'd reached the limit to how far I could go with the information that was within my immediate grasp.

Stage 2: Enter Jordan Peterson

I won't say that I'd mastered TRP by the end of the first six years of the ascent. What I will say, however, is that I'd managed to assimilate CA's ideas and merge them into my understanding of the Biblical narrative. Of course, unlike the Alpe d'Huez climb, where each hairpin turn was numbered, allowing me to monitor my progress, I had no way of knowing how far along I was in this mythological climb. I felt, however, that I was nearing the summit. What I didn't realize was that this summit didn't represent the peak of the climb but rather the limit to how far I could go using only the ideas that I already possessed.

Like a multi-stage rocket, I'd spent all of the motivational fuel in the first stage of the rocket and I needed to switch to or ignite the next stage. In the Alpe d'Huez climb this corresponded to finding a new source of motivation to get to the top, the motivation that I'd started the climb with no longer being sufficient to motivate me to continue. As my mind started to entertain the idea of giving up, my thoughts jumped to a similar challenge that I'd attempted as a teenager.

The challenge I'd set for myself back then was to ride from the Soo to Blind River, a distance of 145 km or 90 miles. I'd headed out rather unprepared, having assumed that the weather would cooperate but it didn't and the ride turned out to be much harder on that account. After a miserable day in the saddle, I finally broke down in Iron Bridge, 25 km short of my destination. When my ride picked me up, however, the weather finally broke and the road went from craggily to smooth, from undulating to flat and from having nearly no shoulder to speak of to a shoulder the width of a car. On seeing this change in conditions, I realized that I'd given up too early. I realized I could have completed the ride if I'd just hung in there. The regret that came from this realization robbed me of any sense of accomplishment on that day despite the fact that I'd still managed to ride 120 km under very poor conditions.

The regret from that early experience came rushing to my rescue as I climbed Alpe d'Huez. The emotional impact that this memory had was to me the ignition of the second stage of the rocket. The emotional fuel from this second stage would carry me almost all the way to the finish line.

In a strikingly similar way, I reached a point in my mythological climb where the fuel from the first stage was now entirely spent and a second stage needed to take over. And just like it had happened in the physical climb, the second stage consisted of a change in motivational force. This transition from the first to the second stage took place precisely four years ago, during the Thanksgiving weekend of 2018. That was when you first appeared on my radar.

The way in which this happened is rather remarkable. It started with a conversation that took place while we, my wife and I, were up visiting her son and his wife. The conversation somehow came around to responsibility and I took advantage of the situation to try to articulate, for the first time, all that I'd learned since I came across CA and TRP. This conversation went on for a couple of hours before taking an abrupt turn. Suddenly both of them started asking me where I got these ideas, and they became quite adamant that the ideas themselves sounded just like those of someone I'd never heard of, someone by the name of Jordan Peterson.

They were rather incredulous when I insisted that I'd never heard of this Peterson guy, whoever he was. For my part, I was just as incredulous about the idea that someone, anyone, might hold a similar view to mine. Regardless, the conversation came to an end and, had it been left entirely to me that would have been the end of it. As fate would have it, though, about a week later they followed up with an email containing a link to your interview with Dr. Oz. That nudge is what got me to turn my attention to this anomalous stranger who supposedly shared the same fundamental ideas about responsibility as I did.

A different form of motivation

I immediately recognized that I'd been wrong and they'd been right. As unbelievable as it was to me, it became abundantly clear that our thinking ran along parallel tracks. In this way, your appearance on my radar constitutes a hairpin bend on my mythological climb. And just as regret fueled the second stage of the physical climb, you and your ideas would provide the motivational fuel that would take me almost to the summit of the mythological ascent.

From the very moment that I recognized the similarities in our thinking, I became convinced that you would want to hear from me, that you would want the opportunity to interact with me. The more I listened to you the more convinced I became. With hindsight I can see that I implicitly understood the significance of my journey and I believed that it was something you would want to know about. I can also see, again only with the benefit of hindsight, that I was premature in thinking this. I've also, since then, become aware of the fact that, just as I was starting to reach out to you, your life was falling into chaos. Nevertheless, I was blind to what was going on in your life and so I was motivated to *reach* you. This is the motivation that that would pull me forward for the next three and a half years, right up to the night that we met, just a few months ago.

I'd taken things as far as I could and then, when there was no way to make any further progress, you "appeared." In that way, Thanksgiving of 2018 represents a dramatic change in motivation, a switch from the first to the second stage of the climb. Movement forward continued uninterrupted and the next hairpin bend to present itself came in the form of something you said during one of your Biblical lectures. The idea had to do with producing a "bad first draft," as you called it. I found this idea so compelling that I immediately set myself to doing just that. I produced this admittedly very bad first draft in three weeks. I tried emailing it to you, but by this point, you'd become so popular that getting through proved impossible. Nevertheless, I'd managed to get my ideas written down and so I now had a skeletal first draft of this book.

I'd actually started writing back in 2011. At first it was a means of working through some personal issues, but as my ascent began, I spent a lot of time trying to organize my thoughts and ideas, those thoughts and ideas that were specific to the ascent. And so, I'd already tried, numerous times in fact, to produce a bad first draft but I simply couldn't find a path through the seemingly infinitely complex network of related ideas that I had accumulated. What made this attempt different from my previous attempts to produce a bad first draft was that, for the first time, I could picture my audience. In all of my previous attempts to produce a bad first draft, I'd gotten bogged down by the problem of what I could and couldn't assume that my audience understood. In writing specifically to you, I'd found a freedom of expression that came from knowing that I didn't need to explain the concepts and ideas that I was playing with because you already understood them. This experience was a breakthrough for me and it lead directly to the next bend in the climb.

The exercise of writing specifically to a single person had provided me with a way of organizing and presenting my thoughts without getting entangled in an endless effort to explain all of the fundamental ideas. Perhaps as a result of this success, soon after this breakthrough an idea came to me. The idea was to repeat the exercise only with a different audience. I would repeat the exercise, only this time, rather than writing to a scientist, I decided I would write to a Christian.

My first book[20]

As I recall I was about halfway through your Biblical lectures when I stopped to produce my terrible first draft. I returned to your lectures on Genesis after I'd completed this little exercise. The idea of repeating the process by writing to a Christian came on the heels of completing the lecture series.

I recognized that a few weeks simply wouldn't be sufficient to this task, and so I decided that I would set aside ninety days in which I would dedicate myself to it. I would get up and write before work and on weekends, and spend my evenings thinking about what I would write the next day. The format that I chose was personal or intimate, as I chose to imagine myself writing to an old friend from my days as a Christian. The idea was that each day I would write him a "letter" and together, the series of letters would provide him with an update with respect to how my thinking, especially about the Bible, had evolved over the ensuing years.

I completed this climb within the climb on schedule. It wasn't pretty, but once again, I was greatly encouraged by the fact that I'd managed to find a way through. After this exercise I became all the more convinced that you'd be interested in what I had to say, and specifically in what I'd just produced even if it was still only a bad first draft. This ascent, and more specifically these writing exercises, were having the effect of bringing something other than my dead father to the surface. As I moved forward, I became aware of an inner sense or implicit understanding that I was beginning to actualize my purpose, and the more explicit this became the more I found myself gripped by a sense of urgency. This sense of urgency compelled me to reach out to

---

20   Jordan B. Peterson: Sinner? By A. Believer

you again, only this time I determined to take a slightly more aggressive approach, one that would at least ensure that I got your attention.

My approach worked, at least in the sense that I did manage to get your attention. It also backfired, however, because you concluded that no one with honorable motives would resort to the means that I used to get your attention. The end result was that you threatened me with legal action, strongly recommend that I seek professional help, and slammed the door shut. In an act of desperation and almost petrified that you would actually take legal action against me, I decided to (self) publish this draft and to do so in such a way as to try to provoke you to read it. What I mean by that is that I chose a provocative title and added a rather overly confrontational introduction in which I accepted your challenge, the one I saw clearly proclaimed in your video "Who Dares Say He Believes in God?"[21] I also made one other modification to the book.

I'd started listening to MoM for the first time immediately after I'd finished drafting the book and the new introduction. There were a number of illustrations that I still needed to generate before I could publish it, and it was during this time that I turned to MoM. Everything I heard you say only reinforced my implicit belief that you would want to hear from me. I hadn't even finished listening to the book when I felt compelled to add a closing chapter that, like the introduction, was written directly to you. I mention all of this for two reasons. First, this book constitutes a sort of snapshot of my thinking prior to being exposed to your ideas. What's more, the closing chapter that I added points you, directs you to look to JG's *Chaos*. The value of this draft, then, lies in the fact that it shows the direction I was moving in. What's more, it demonstrates that I gave you the opportunity to make the discovery yourself, had you but paid attention to what I had to say.

This book was all that, but for me it was also the end of the line. I had gone as far as I could with the ideas that I had already accumulated. I may have been pointed in the right direction but it felt like standing on one side

---

21   https://youtu.be/MnUfXYGtT5Q

of the Grand Canyon and pointing to the other side and saying that's where I have to go. As far as I was concerned, I wasn't capable of crossing that divide. I didn't know and had no way of knowing that I would need to study your ideas for a year before I would be able to take another step forward. At least now, however, I had you giving me insights into what I was doing. Through MoM I came to realize that this ascent constituted a mythological climb, and for the first time, I got a sense of where I was in my journey:

> Dorn's ideas refer to a conjunction conceptualized as a three-stage process. The first stage was "union of the mind" (the "overcoming the body by mental union"). This stage refers to the integration of "states of motivation" (drives, emotions) into a single hierarchy, dominated by the figure of the exploratory hero. The second stage was (re)union of the united mind with the body. This was equivalent to the second stage of the hero's journey. After the treasure is released, consequential to the battle with the dragon, the purely personal aspect of the hero's journey is completed. After all, he has found the "treasure hard to attain." But the second stage of the hero's journey is return to the community.

I realized when I came across this idea in MoM that I'd completed the first stage in my journey, the *purely personal aspect* of my journey. This might have come as good news if it weren't for the fact that the ascent wouldn't be over until I managed my *return to the community*. What's worse, the more I thought about this the more I became convinced that the only chance I had of a return to community was through you. I knew of nobody else whose thinking was anywhere near mine, and so it seemed to me that the only way to successfully return to community was through you.

I won't get into the details, but I spent the next year trying to get your attention, or more specifically, trying to find a way to get you to read my book. From my perspective I was at an impasse. I couldn't move forward because I'd taken my ideas as far as I possibly could. The only way forward seemed to be through you, and so that became my primary focus. This preoccupation, however, had a beneficial side effect, and that was that it kept me digging into MoM. For more than a year, I dove ever deeper into MoM as I continued my feeble attempts to find a way through the fortified walls that surrounded you. It's quite likely that I would have remained stuck in this pattern of behavior if it weren't for the next hairpin bend on the ascent.

That bend came in the form of Covid-19.

The final leg of the ascent

When Covid-19 broke out, I was forced to conclude that it was now completely inappropriate for me to continue using the tactics that I'd been using to try to get your attention, and with that realization, I abandoned all attempts to reach you. This, of course, sent me back to the drawing board, as they say. And so I returned to consider my bad first draft.

I'd never felt good about the introduction that I'd written in an attempt to provoke you, and so I determined to update it to something that came closer to the mark. This decision to rewrite the introduction lead me to reconsider the final chapter that I'd tacked onto the end of the book as well. As a result, I found myself following the instructions that I'd written for you and I returned to JG's *Chaos* once again. Only by this time, I had become very familiar with your ideas and so when I got to the section on the Mandelbrot set, I could see the connections between your conception of Christ and the process that renders the Mandelbrot set visible. In this way, what began as an intention to rewrite the introduction turned into a complete rewrite.

Thanks to Covid-19, I found myself forced to continue on my own; but thanks to the effort that I'd put into contending with your ideas during the year or so after writing my first book, I now had new ideas to process and assimilate, and that's what motivated me during the next leg of my ascent.

The ascent was now about this book. I managed to capture all of the essential ideas, but the further I went the more formidable the challenge became. I found myself hitting a wall. I could see from the draft that was emerging and the effort that it required that I had years of climbing ahead of me if things continued at this pace and I became concerned, if not convinced, that I would never be able to finish. That's when I became aware of some new dates that you'd added to your *Beyond Order* book tour, and with that my attention turned, once again, to connecting with you, only this time I was armed with a clear picture of your conception of Christ.

I decided that I would create the opportunity to provide you with a copy of this draft in person. And so, I purchased VIP tickets that would allow me the opportunity to speak to you face to face. That brings us to the night that we met. Surprisingly enough, there's an element of the physical ascent that corresponds to this quite nicely.

Even the intense desire not to quit too early knowing the regret I'd have to live with wasn't enough to pull me all the way to the finish line. With only a few hundred meters between me and the finish line, I reached an end within myself. I suspect I would have quit with only this short distance left to go if it weren't for this parking lot that appeared on the right hand side of the road. Unable to go any further, I turned into that parking lot, the first level ground I'd encountered since the climb began. I didn't get off my bike but just rode to the end of the lot trying to find some sort of hidden reserve that I could use to finish the climb. I found that reserve in a glimpse of the finish line, which was visible from the end of this parking lot.

To be clear, it wasn't the sight of the finish line that motivated me. It was the sight of my wife waiting for me at that finish line that did it. On catching a glimpse of her I turned and headed back to the entrance to that parking lot, steeled myself, and pushed myself up those last few meters of this utterly grueling climb.

The evening that we met has turned out to be like that detour into the parking lot. I turned in believing I could never make to the end on my own. That's how I felt leading up to the night of the event. I felt I could never complete this journey on my own. I was turning to you, hoping that it would mean the end of the grueling mythological climb that had already lasted ten years. More accurately, though, when I failed to connect with you I felt as I had when I'd turned off into that parking lot. I felt it was over.

But then I caught a glimpse of something, something that corresponded to the glimpse I'd gotten of my wife waiting at the finish line. And with that, I steeled myself and began the final few meters of my mythological ascent. I was still certain that I couldn't finish the draft that I'd started, so I started over from scratch, keeping only the most vital ideas from the draft that I'd brought to give to you.

From the time that you first appeared on my radar, I've been operating from an implicit belief that you would want to hear from me. Perhaps at a deeper level, I've been operating from the belief that I needed your help in order to succeed in my purpose. Regardless, these assumptions, whether true or false, have kept me in orbit around your ideas for four years now, starting on Thanksgiving weekend of 2018 and ending on the corresponding weekend four years later. And, now that I've reached my finish line, I see that it wasn't you that I needed but your ideas. Without your ideas, without your conception of Christ, I could never have made it to the finish line.

So, when I walked onto that stage, shook your hand, looked you in the eye, and told you that I had come to thank you, it was specifically for the help that you've unknowingly provided me over the past four years. While my real-life interactions with you, on the two occasions when I managed to capture your attention, have left a bad impression on me, your avatar in the form of your books and online lectures has been my constant companion and even my guide over the steepest part of the ascent, and for that I will always be grateful.

Aim at something "lofty"

> *SH - There is a profound net negative that we are paying the*
> *price for every day by believing in paradise, right? A belief that*
> *this life probably doesn't matter very much at all because we get*
> *what we really want after we die is, forget about the evidentiary*
> *basis for that belief; it is ruinous for prioritizing what we should*
> *be prioritizing in this life.*
>
> *JP - I agree with that, by the way.*[22]

Jordan, you make a lot of the idea of aiming at the highest good. In *Beyond Order* you illustrate this idea with a bricklayer who's building a cathedral whose purpose is *"the glorification of the Highest Good."* Now the marvelous thing about most cathedrals is that they tended to be built over the course of centuries. If we imagine that this bricklayer is working on this cathedral in the earlier stages, then he is literally working on a project that will only be completed at some point in the future that lies beyond his death. Is this bricklayer wasting his life toiling on something he will never see completed? More to the point, when you advise your reader to *"Aim at something profound and noble and lofty"* do you mean by that that they should always aim at something profoundly noble and lofty but only so long as they themselves can reap the fruit of their labors and striving? If a cathedral is worth pouring your life's energy into, even though you'll never see it completed, why then is orienting yourself toward "paradise," which I can only assume constitutes a *noble and lofty* goal, something that you consider to constitute "a profound net negative?"

Here's another question. The bricklayer who's working on the cathedral in its early days, do you think that he's going to bring his B-game to this task or his A-game? If he's not going to see the final result, why should he pour his best into this work? What motivation does he have for doing his very best work seeing as the project will only be completed after he's dead? And,

---

if you can imagine this bricklayer doing his very best work on this cathedral, then why exactly is it that A Believer who is oriented toward something that will not be fully materialized until long after he is dead, is acting in a *ruinous* way? Wouldn't you think that, like the bricklayer, aiming at a lofty goal that will not be completed in his lifetime would motivate him to live his best life, to play his A-game?

> 8 *By faith Abraham, when he was called to go out into a place which he should after receive for an inheritance, obeyed; and he went out, not knowing whither he went. 9 By faith he sojourned in the land of promise, as in a strange country, dwelling in tabernacles with Isaac and Jacob, the heirs with him of the same promise: 10 For he looked for a city which hath foundations, whose builder and maker is God...*

> 13 *These all died in faith, not having received the promises, but having seen them afar off, and were persuaded of them, and embraced them, and confessed that they were strangers and pilgrims on the earth. 14 For they that say such things declare plainly that they seek a country. 15 And truly, if they had been mindful of that country from whence they came out, they might have had opportunity to have returned. 16 But now they desire a better country, that is, an heavenly: wherefore God is not ashamed to be called their God: for he hath prepared for them a city.*

> – Hebrews 11:8-10

As a Christian, I believed in heaven, or paradise. I can honestly say that, in a sense, SH is correct. I did, in fact, *ruin* my life by orienting myself towards something that lay somewhere in the future beyond death. I'm quickly approaching sixty and remain, as of yet, unsuccessful. My financial future is entirely uncertain. My *standing* in this world is precarious at best. All of this is a direct result of the twenty years I spent oriented toward heaven. In a very literal sense, then, I have sacrificed my life, my life in this "world." According to both you and SH, I oriented myself incorrectly in this world, but if I'd have done otherwise, I could never have embarked on the hero's journey that has lead me here.

I've heard you say, with respect to this idea of diving into the void and rescuing our dead father, that you fear that we've lost the *technology*, as it were. Nevertheless, I've followed the very steps you lay out so clearly in MoM, which is to say, I've used the very technology that you describe. I've spent decades exposed to a host of Christian symbolism in the Catholic tradition. I've spent another couple of decades in voluntary apprenticeship to Christ. I've ventured to the bottom of the ultimate abyss and battled the ultimate monster and I've returned with treasure in hand, treasure that corresponds precisely with what you would expect from such a journey. I've found my dead Father, revivified Him, and brought him back to the surface. I've united, at least within my *single breast*, Osiris and Horus. And my reward? Well, as it stands right now, I remain stranded on the outside of my culture's walls, apparently insane. Nevertheless, here I stand.

What's more, it seems to me that you should have been expecting a cultural revolutionary hero to emerge. I don't say this merely for the obvious reason, the fact that the revolutionary hero is one of the particular forms of anomaly and therefore may appear in the world of experience, which is to say, real life. In MoM you open section 5.4.2., The Divinity of Interest, with a quote by Jung who, writing about Gnostic philosophy, states:

> *It was founded on the perception of symbols thrown up by the unconscious individuation process which always sets in when the collective dominants of human life fall into decay. At such a time there is bound to be a considerable number of individuals who are possessed by archetypes of a numinous nature that force their way to the surface in order to form new dominants.*
>
> *This state of possession shows itself almost without exception in the fact that the possessed identify themselves with the archetypal contents of their unconscious, and, because they do not realize that the role which is being thrust upon them is the effect of new*

contents still to be understood, they exemplify these concretely in their own lives, thus becoming prophets and reformers.

– Maps of Meaning

It seems to me that it's all right there. We currently live in "such a time" where the "collective dominants of human life [are falling] into decay." At such a time we should expect that "a considerable number of individuals" should "become possessed by archetypes of a numinous nature." When we add to that the fact that "Christ's life and words [are] archetypal exemplars of the heroic manner of being," it isn't hard to see that I happen to be one such individual and the archetype that I was possessed by was that of the archetypal hero, Christ. Regardless, however, the fact remains that you should have known to be on alert for the emergence of the revolutionary hero, and more specifically the cultural revolutionary hero, because it's what your theory predicts.

Conclusion

I want to return to the very final *"leg"* of the ascent, the part that corresponds to the final few hundred meters. I mentioned that in the physical climb, the thing that got me to the finish line was that I'd "caught a glimpse" of my wife waiting for me there. I also mentioned that in the mythological climb a similar "glimpse" of something was responsible for getting me to the finish line. As we are now crossing that finish line, I'd like to share with you what it was that I caught a glimpse of after I'd lost my opportunity to "transmit" what I'd learned to you in person.

In the previous chapter we explored some core doctrines in the Protestant faith. We mentioned the doctrines of "total depravity," "limited atonement," and "unconditional election." These doctrines, along with two others, "irresistible grace" and the "perseverance of the saints," constitute what are known as the "doctrines of grace" or the "five points of Calvinism." These doctrines constitute the very core of Protestant faith. These doctrines were so central to the Reformation that both Luther and Calvin were of one mind on this matter. These five doctrines, the Doctrines of Grace, constitute the very heart of the evangelical Gospel:

> *It starts with man in need of salvation (Total depravity) and then gives, in the order of their occurrence, the steps God takes to save his people. He elects (Unconditional election), then he sends Jesus to atone for the sins of the elect (Limited atonement), then he irresistibly draws his people to faith (Irresistible grace), and finally works to cause them to persevere to the end (Perseverance of the saints).*
>
> – John Piper[23]

While I'm not a fan of labels, I became a "five-point Calvinist," a Christian who holds all five of these doctrines as Biblical truth. So, when I walked away from God I was faced with a particularly troubling implication to my actions. I knew I was walking away from God, which meant I was "dropping out" or not "persevering," which could only mean one thing, that I'd never really been a true Christian in the first place (1 John 2:19). I was forced to this conclusion even though I couldn't for the life of me see that I had been anything but genuine in my love toward God and Christ. Nevertheless, the doctrine was clear, so when I walked away I assumed that it meant that I had never really been a true believer.

While I had prayed for years, offering myself up to do whatever God wanted of me, it never entered into my mind that God would call me to walk away from Him in order to lead me down into the depths of "hell" in order to find my dead Father and bring Him back to the surface. As I mentioned earlier, I started the ascent by taking responsibility for the self-fulfilling prophecy problem in order to see where following The Responsibility Process would lead me. Through this process, I zigzagged my way all the way up to the night we met. The disappointment that came from watching you walk

---

23   https://www.desiringgod.org/articles/what-we-believe-about-the-five-points-of-calvinism

off that stage and not give me a second thought served to turn my gaze away from "man" and that's when I caught a glimpse of God's hand in all of this.

The empty stage represented the empty parking lot that held nothing for me but failure. But then I glimpsed God standing at the finish line of my mythological climb in much the same way that I'd glimpsed my wife standing at the finish line at the top of Alpe d'Huez. In both cases, what made the difference between getting to or falling short of the finish line, was love, love of my wife and love of God.

While it's likely that no doctrinally sound Christian would accept me as a Christian, I see God's hand in all of this. As a Christian, I understood that I had a purpose but that that purpose might never be revealed to me. When I jumped into the nihilistic void, I lost all sense of purpose, meaning, and hope. After discovering my dead father and bringing Him back to the surface, I now see that God answered the prayers that I'd uttered as a Christian and He used me as He pleased. And so, I can see that in praying the prayers that I prayed, I had volunteered for this "mission." And while there is a discontinuity between my former "Christian self" and my current self, my story is no longer a mess of disjointed pieces but is now as straight as an arrow and all honour and glory belong to God.

It is God who raised me up to be the first to recognize the "revelation" of Christ, but I couldn't have seen this if it weren't for the fact that God raised you up to produce MoM and catapulted you into the stratosphere so that you would come to my attention when I was ready. It's also God that raised CA up to produce *The Responsibility Process*. And it doesn't stop there. JG's *Chaos* is another critical element without which I wouldn't have succeeded. And there are countless others who fit into the causal chain that led to this recognition, too many to mention here for sure. And all of these had to come into play in just the right way and at just the right time. God, "what calls and what responds in the eternal call to adventure," has called each of us separately and given us each a part to play, but it remains that God orchestrated the whole thing.

In closing, I would like to leave you with two imagistic representations that summarize what we've covered about God's "plan of salvation." The first image corresponds to salvation as it applies to the individual. The second represents the "big picture" view of God's plan. In both cases we're going to use CA's chart as the "foundation."

In both cases we're going to want to pay careful attention to the double line in the chart. In the first image, we're going to treat this double line as a symbolic representation of death or our own individual mortality. The idea of death, of course, is present in the idea of a paradigm shift. In the case of TRP, for instance, we can think of embodying Responsibility as corresponding to the death of Coping. Understanding this paradigm shift is therefore critical to a correct understanding of CA's conception of Responsibility.

So, let's take a step back in order to build a more substantial understanding of what that double line represents. Fundamentally, this line constitutes a discontinuity between two different ways of perceiving the same information. This line is imaginary meaning it can never be observed directly. To help us see this line for what it is, let's consider the Necker cube.[24] There are only two valid ways of construing this cube, and so we can imagine a line that separates the two "interpretations" of the information. But since this line corresponds to death, let's switch to a similar optical illusion, one in which there are only two valid interpretations and which also includes an emotional element. For this, we'll use the "My Wife and My Mother-in-Law"[25] image, which can be seen as either "attractive" or "repulsive." Visualizing the "hag" or "mother-in-law" in this image corresponds to the fear of death. We don't want to look at it.

Let's extend this idea of having two valid ways of construing the ambiguous information contained in both these optical illusions. Let's return to JG's *Chaos* in order to see how systems demonstrate the same fundamental "bivalent" personality:

---

24   Necker cube. In Wikipedia. https://en.wikipedia.org/wiki/Necker_cube

25   My Wife and My Mother-in-Law. In Wikipedia. https://en.wikipedia.org/wiki/My_Wife_and_My_Mother-in-Law

Hiding within a particular system could be more than one stable solution. An observer might see one kind of behavior over a very long time, yet a completely different kind of behavior could be just as natural for the system. Such a system is called intransitive. It can stay in one equilibrium or the other, but not both. Only a kick from outside can force it to change states.

– Chaos

If we imagine that our double line serves to differentiate between the two *completely different kinds of behavior* that constitute the two stable solutions of an intransitive system, we can see your *two transpersonal patterns of behavior and schemas of representation, comprising the individual.*

Keeping in mind that an intransitive system can only express one of these two states at a time and that the system remains locked in on one particular state until it receives a "kick from outside" we can now "see" something that corresponds to the Biblical idea of salvation.

The Biblical idea of salvation can be correctly thought of in terms of an intransitive system. The "world" constitutes "one kind of behavior" while the "kingdom of God" constitutes a completely different "kind of behavior." Extending this idea just a bit, let's assume that the world and the kingdom of God are two separate and distinct cultures. Because people adapt to their environment, placing the individual within one of these cultures will produce a certain kind of behavior. Taking an individual and moving them from one culture to the other corresponds to an external kick, which will result in the individual demonstrating an entirely different kind of behavior. Correctly understanding the Biblical conception of salvation should be easy for you if you recognize that the default culture is the world. Salvation, Biblical salvation, corresponds to being "moved" from one culture to the other: "Who hath delivered us from the power of darkness, and hath translated us into the kingdom of his dear Son" (Colossians 1:13).

We're getting close to having a clear understanding of what Biblical salvation represents. But there's one more idea or concept that we need in order to fully understand Biblical salvation and especially the doctrine of perseverance of the saints, and that idea has to do with "mode locking."

> *This phenomenon, in which one regular cycle locks into another, is now called entrainment, or mode locking. Mode locking explains why the moon always faces the earth, or more generally why satellites tend to spin in some whole-number ratio of their orbital period: 1 to 1, or 2 to 1, or 3 to 2. When the ratio is close to a whole number, nonlinearity in the tidal attraction of the satellite tends to lock it in. Mode locking occurs throughout electronics, making it possible, for example, for a radio receiver to lock in on signals even when there are small fluctuations in their frequency. Mode locking accounts for the ability of groups of oscillators, including biological oscillators, like heart cells and nerve cells, to work in synchronization.*
>
> *– Chaos*

We can "see" this mode locking at work within us by looking at one of our optical illusions. Each of the valid ways of construing the information presented in those illusions constitutes a stable solution to the problem of ambiguity. When your mind switches from one interpretation to another, it is behaving like an intransitive system that been given a kick. But once we "see" one of the valid "solutions," our minds lock in on that solution.

Salvation can correctly be understood along these lines except it requires a couple of clarifying points. The first is that we all start off expressing the default state, the state in which we have no adaptive structure with respect to God or death. The Gospel then is the force that kicks the individual causing him to be "translated" or shifted from the culture that "the world" constitutes into the culture or "kingdom of genuine identity." The "kick" represents the impact that "Irresistible Grace" exerts on the individual such that he is pulled and not pushed into the kingdom of genuine identity. This of course indicates that there is an element of voluntary response built into the process of salvation. Once "saved" in this way, "mode locking" takes over and the individual then "perseveres" in this new state.

With all of these ideas under our belt, let's turn to the first of the two illustrations I'd like to leave you with.

Image 11: Individual "salvation"[26]

---

26   **Background Image:** The Responsibility Process Poster © The Responsibility Company

This work is licensed under the creative commons attribution-noderivatives 4.0 international license. To view a copy of this license, visit creativecommons.org/licenses/by-nd/4.0/

TRP®-POSTER-USA-DEC2021.PDF

Allow me to draw your attention to the key elements in this image. First, I've added a black "pyramid" to CA's chart. This pyramid represents the value hierarchy that constitutes "the World." Note that this image is ambiguous and the pyramid can also be seen as a road. This road stands in contrast to the "straight and narrow path" that leads to Responsibility, and so this illustrates Christ's words from Matthew: *Enter ye in at the strait gate: for wide is the gate, and broad is the way, that leadeth to destruction, and many there be which go in thereat* (Matthew 7:13). What's more, we can see that the straight and narrow way "passes through" death, through the double lines. What this represents is the believer setting his sights on a goal that is so lofty that it lies beyond death. The salient point here is that forward is defined as somewhere beyond death. The person on the narrow path looks "through" death and is therefore "death facing."

Taking a careful look at the broad path, we see that it never really faces death. Like most people, it looks like it will face death somewhere down the road but there's no indication from the diagram that it ever will. The individual on the broad path can focus his attention on "the things of this world" and ignore, deny, and even try to cheat death. The salient point is that forward is defined differently on the broad path. Whatever forward is, it is isn't death-facing. And so, I've placed an image of the cross where the narrow path intersects with "death" as a reminder that it is Christ's death and identification with His death that transforms the individual's attitude toward death, and of course, God. *For I determined not to know anything among you, save Jesus Christ, and him crucified* (1 Corinthians 2:2).

Now that we've illustrated the Biblical idea of personal or individual salvation, let's turn our attention to the second image which we'll use to illustrate God's plan of salvation for the world. We might call this God's plan of salvation for humanity. To illustrate this, we're going to turn CA's chart on its side. Next we'll add a timeline to the chart and position it such that it sits directly on top of the narrow path. With the timeline in place we'll add a couple of symbols to represent the two historical events that the

New Testament is a description of. These two events, as we've seen, are the crucifixion and the marriage of the Lamb of God.

The marriage of the Lamb is equivalent to the return of Christ, which corresponds to the emergence of "what Christ represents" out of the obscurity of implicit knowledge into the light as a fully explicitly declared idea. This is literally the "Revelation of Christ," which I've represented on the timeline using the illustration of the "wedding ring" that we've been using to represents the marriage of Christ to His Bride. The "world" is represented in this illustration using the same pyramid that constitutes the value hierarchy of the world "system." Viewing this pyramid as a road, we now see just how much the two paths diverge. In the previous image, you might have been tempted to conclude that both roads led to approximately the same destination, but in this image we can see that the world and the kingdom of God run counter to each other, at cross-purposes to each other. More importantly, however, when we lay it out this way, we can see that, in setting their sights on "heaven," the believer is setting his sights on an event in the distant future. The Christian has been aiming at something in the distant future in much the same way that the bricklayer aims at the completion of a cathedral that won't be finished till after he's dead.

Looking forward to this event, Paul writes, *Behold, I shew you a mystery; We shall not all sleep, but we shall all be changed*" (1 Corinthians 15:51). Of course, by "we shall not all sleep" Paul means we shall not all die. This means that some people will be alive when this change takes place. What's more, now that Christ has become visible, it is correct to say that this event is upon us and we are about to see God's plan come to fruition. Note that I've drawn a vertical line over the double line on the chart. This line intersects the timeline at the marriage of the Lamb. Following that line all the way to the bottom we see that the tip of the pyramid stops short of that line that signifies the end of the world and the beginning of a new heaven and new earth, a new world.

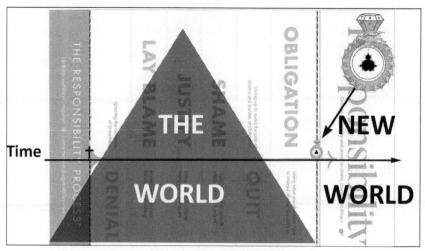

Image 12: World "salvation"[27]

This illustration serves to illustrate something else, something significant. We've mentioned that salvation plays itself out in time. With the timeline in place, we have illustrated here the path of every Christian. It starts at the narrow gate, the foot of the cross. From there, the Christian must "walk in the world." *I pray not that thou shouldest take them out of the world, but that thou shouldest keep them from the evil"* (John 17:15). The Christian enters at the straight gate and is to "persevere" or remain on the narrow path till death or the "return" of Christ, the marriage of the Lamb. The believer must therefore walk, or live his life, within a culture whose value hierarchy is different from the culture he has been "translated" into. This means that he is continually subjected to the expectations of the dominant culture. He is to remain on the path and not be conformed to this world but be transformed and thereby demonstrate that his culture is the culture of genuine identity.

Together, these two images represent God's plan of salvation in its entirety. It encompasses both the individual and the "world." God works

27   **Background Image:** The Responsibility Process Poster © The Responsibility Company

This work is licensed under the creative commons attribution-noderivatives 4.0 international license. To view a copy of this license, visit creativecommons.org/licenses/by-nd/4.0/

TRP®-POSTER-USA-DEC2021.PDF

through the individual, the locus of experience, to transform him, to mold and shape him into the image of "God's Son." This change to the "constituent atoms" within the dynamic system of culture alters the behavior of these "atoms" or individuals and this becomes the means of transforming the culture. But the culture is like an intransitive system that continues to produce a certain kind of behavior until it receives an external "kick" to cause it to switch over to an entirely different type of behavior. This change in the culture's "equilibrium" constitutes both the destruction, or at least the death of "the world," and marriage of the Lamb simultaneously. And so, these two images illustrate the central ideas articulated in the Biblical narrative.

I now stand an arm's length from the finish line. I've been compelled all the way along by a sense of urgency, and that will remain until I've published this book. Ever since Covid-19 came onto the scene, I have been haunted by the idea that I could die before completing my journey, and for the first time since I started this ascent ten years ago, I feel that God will allow me to complete my mission. I have now "transmitted" the vital information that constitutes my "treasure in hand." Once this is published, I will finally be able to rest knowing that I have lived the life of A True Believer. I have prioritized the kingdom of God (Matthew 6:33) in my own life and even sacrificed my life in this world in order to follow God's call both to discipline and adventure. I have walked away from God only to discover that He sustains and guides even when He hides His face from you. He preserves those who are His even if he calls them to walk through the valley of the shadow of death. And, while I realize that God owes me nothing and may very well bring my story to an end once this book is published, it's my hope that I will be granted one final chapter in which I can watch as the world is transformed into "a city in which righteousness dwells."

With gratitude for all your help in getting to the finish line,

Anonymous Believer

If the exploratory figure has in fact derived a new mode of adaptation or representation, necessary for the continued success and survival of the group, substantial social change is inevitable.

– Maps of Meaning